Fruitful or Unfruitful?
Why It *Really* Matters

Edward N. Gross

Foreword from
Dawson Trotman
Founder of the Navigators

Fruitful or Unfruitful? Why It Really Matters

ISBN: Softcover 978-1-949888-32-4

Copyright © 2017 by Edward N. Gross

All rights reserved. No part of this book may be reproduced or transmitted in any form or by any means, electronic or mechanical, including photocopying, recording, or by any information storage and retrieval system, without permission in writing from the publisher.

All Scripture quotations, unless otherwise indicated, are taken from the English Standard Version Bible copyright 2001 by Crossway, a publishing ministry of Good News Publishers.

To order additional copies of this book, contact:

Parson's Porch Books
1-423-475-7308
www.parsonsporch.com

Parson's Porch Books is an imprint of **Parson's Porch & Book Publishers** in Cleveland, Tennessee, which has double focus. We focus on the needs of creative writers who need a professional publisher to get their work to market, & we also focus on the needs of others by sharing our profits with those who struggle in poverty to meet their basic needs of food, clothing, shelter and safety.

Fruitful or Unfruitful?

Dedication

*I lovingly dedicate this to my brothers
Ralph, David, John and Strother Gross,
with the prayer that they will always follow Jesus
by lives of great compassion and fruitfulness*

Contents

Foreword 9

Preface 11

1 - God's First Command 15

2 - Fishers of Men 21

3 - Foolish or Wise? 27

4 - Good and Faithful Servant? 35

5 - Who is on God's Side? 45

6 - When filled with the Spirit you will … 53

7 - I Looked for Fruit 61

8 - Sowing and Reaping in the Old Testament 69

9 - Cut it Down! 79

10 - Sowing and Reaping in the Gospels 85

11 - Good or Bad Soil? 95

12 - Your Kingdom Come… 101

13 - Christ's Final Command 107

Appendix 1 115

Appendix 2 119

Appendix 3 123

Appendix 4 126

Appendix 5 131

Foreword from
"Born to Reproduce"

At the close of his life, in 1955, Dawson Trotman, founder of the Navigators, delivered a powerful and significant message that was later printed and widely distributed as, "Born to Reproduce." In it he made many significant and revealing points, including the following:

"Five years ago, Billy Graham came to me and said, 'Daws, we would like you to help with our follow-up.... We are having an average of 6,000 people come forward to decide for Christ in a month's campaign. I feel that with the work you have done you could come in and help us." I said, "Billy, I can't follow up 6,000 people. My work is always with individuals and small groups. "Look, Daws," he answered, 'everywhere I go I meet Navigators. I met them in school in Wheaton. They are in my school right now. (He was president of Northwestern Schools at that time.) There must be something to this." "I just don't have the time," I said. He tackled me again. The third time he pled with me and said, "Daws, I am not able to sleep nights for thinking of what happens to the converts after a crusade is over."

"Some time ago I (Trotman) talked to 29 missionary candidates. They were graduates of universities or Bible Schools or Seminaries. As a member of the board I interviewed each one over a period of five days, giving each candidate from half an hour to an hour.... I asked them, 'You are going out to the foreign field. You hope to be used by the Lord in winning men and women to Christ. Is that right?' 'Yes.' 'You want them to go on and live the victorious life, don't you? You don't want them just to make a decision and then go back into the world, do you?' 'Then may I ask you something more? How many persons do you know by name today who were won to Christ by you and are living for Him?' The majority had to admit that they were ready to cross an ocean and learn a foreign language, but they had not won their first soul who was going on with Jesus Christ. A number of them said that they got many people to go to church; others said they had persuaded some to go forward when the invitation was given. I asked, 'Are they living for Christ now?' Their eyes dropped. I then continued, 'How do you expect that by crossing an ocean and speaking in a foreign language with people who are suspicious of you, whose way of life is unfamiliar, you will be able to do there what you have not yet done here?'"

"Wherever you find a Christian who is not leading men and women to Christ, something is wrong. He may still be a babe. I do not mean that he does not know a lot of doctrine and is not well informed through hearing good preaching. I know many people who can argue the Pre-, the post- and the-A-millennial position ... but who are still immature.... Are you producing? If not, why not'? Is it because of a lack of communion with Christ, your Lord, that closeness of fellowship which is part of the great plan? Or is it some sin in your life, an unconfessed something, that has stopped the flow? Or is it that you are still a babe? 'For when for the time ye ought to be teachers, ye have need that one teaches you again.' (Hebrews *5:12).* Because they were babes, they were immature, incapable of spiritual reproduction. In other words, they could not help other people to be born again." [Anyone can listen to, or download, Trotman's entire message at www.Discipleshiplibrary.com

– From **Dawson Trotman's "Born to Reproduce"** (1955)

Preface

I am writing this book to prove that Trotman's premise was right and to warn Christians of the danger of forgetting the truth that we are "Born to Reproduce." I want to show that the believers who have courageously witnessed, hymn writers who sang, missionaries who went, evangelists who proclaimed and authors who wrote about winning the lost at all cost cannot possibly all be wrong!

In this book I am sharing one basic truth: God saves us to transform us into Christ's image and to flow through us in the saving of others. This truth is so important to God that He mentions it over and over again in the Bible. It can hardly be missed, unless you have become blinded to it. And that can happen when we allow something else to take its place. Unfortunately, many western Christians no longer believe that a saved person must be a witness of Christ. Wrong conclusions about being "saved by grace" and being objects of "the love of God," have led many to a selfish, comfortable, passive lifestyle of unfruitfulness.

Many Christians have focused so totally on family, home, job, country, church and each other—that they have forgotten the last great words of their Lord Jesus. With those words He focused His disciples' attention on beginning at home and then going worldwide doing two chief things: proclaiming the gospel and making disciples by the power of the Holy Spirit. This command was originally obeyed and passed on to subsequent generations. It was modeled, written about and repeated in many different ways. As we will see, our duty and privilege to bear spiritual children is echoed throughout the Holy Scriptures.

Initially, I need to make three things clear. First, I am **NOT** saying only soul-winners go to heaven. There are some providential exceptions. But, I am affirming that, normally, every follower of Jesus will eventually take some part in the harvest of souls. A major goal of Christ is that every follower of His would be a witness and disciple maker. So, when we turn away from that, we have, at that moment, actually stopped following Jesus. You should not plan on being an exception to the call and work of Christ.

Secondly, I am **NOT** advocating "salvation by works." We are saved by God's grace through the faith that He graciously gives us in Christ. However, I am affirming that true saving faith does eventually produce a changed life. And one clear evidence of having spiritual life or being born again is the desire and determination to see others saved from death and hell, too.

Thirdly, by my title, I am **NOT** saying that all uses of the words fruit, fruitful, sow, reap and harvest in the Bible refer to reproduction. Fruit, in the Bible, may refer to what someone does, or to someone's moral or spiritual character, or to the reward that someone gets from their efforts or lives. Each biblical context will determine the precise meaning of what "fruit" and other "agricultural" terms mean in that passage.

What I am trying to make clear is that there are many indisputable passages where fruit means that which is actually reproduced. Children are "the fruit" of their parents. They literally carry the DNA of mom and dad. Throughout the Bible, God calls His children (those bearing His spiritual nature and following Him) to reproduce and have spiritual children. My focus is on those texts. What they clearly state may be either encouraging or frightening to you. They were designed to produce whatever change and action are needed for us to get to the real work of advancing God's Kingdom. If you call yourself a Christian, and your life is **not** producing faith in others, is not seeing others believe and become disciples, then the Scripture reveals that you are truly in danger. I pray that the words that follow will help change and re-focus your life.

I am not going to attempt to establish my premise by a long and careful exegesis of each passage to which I allude. That is not needed. To do so would be to unnecessarily lengthen the book and to obscure the light of this simple, single truth from shining clearly. God saves us to serve Him by helping to save others. I hope, as you read through the many texts to follow, you will "get it," and be a loving disciple of Jesus obsessed with fulfilling His Great Commission.

-Edward (Ed) Gross (2017)

"I firmly believe that the biggest challenge remains REPRODUCTION. Our biggest challenge in sharing the Gospel to the unreached is not to make converts, but to make disciples that will REPRODUCE."

-Mike Burnard (The 18 Inch Principle) 2011

Chapter 1
God's First Command

After creating Adam and Eve, the Lord God issued a clear command. "Be fruitful and multiply" (Genesis 1:28). Have you ever considered what might have happened if Adam and Eve had disobeyed that command? If they had not reproduced? Had they just thought, "We are quite happy here alone with each other." The two of us walking with God. Why must we complicate matters? This is perfect. We are supremely happy—alone with Him.

But, they were created to reproduce. The very way God fashioned the male and female bodies was to encourage intimate, physical reproduction. We were designed by Him to have a personal, face-to-face encounter of love.

It was impossible for Adam and Eve to deny their reproductive nature —apart from the entrance of sin. They loved God. They were made to duplicate. And He commanded them to do so. But they hesitated.

For a moment, please seriously consider how Adam and Eve did something awful when they began listening to the devil while gazing at the forbidden fruit on the Tree of the Knowledge of Good and Evil. In those moments, they considered something that utterly changed them and horribly altered the course of all human history. They listened to the devil, took it and ate it. Perhaps they should have been doing what God commanded them to do. Maybe they should have been enjoying each other and reproducing! We often get into a lot of trouble when we do not quickly obey God by simply doing what He has said.

What if?

Their first offspring, Cain, was conceived (Genesis 4) after Adam & Eve fell into sin (Genesis 3). We cannot calculate how long a time elapsed between God's initial command to reproduce and the time that Cain was conceived. What we do know is that he was born with a sinful nature. His start was worlds different from that of his parents. What a miserable life was Cain's. Ask yourself, "How different would it have been had his parents put first things first and done what God commanded?" Instead they did what He had forbidden!

How different the temptation of the serpent would have appeared if Adam & Eve had a baby, born pure, sinless and devoted to God—and THEN been tempted to sin by eating the forbidden fruit.

Genesis 2:6 may have gone like this. "So when the woman saw that the tree was good for food, and that it was delightful to the eyes, and that the tree was to be desired to make one wise, she took of its fruit and" ... looked at her baby and thought, "What am I doing? How can I disobey the God that gave me this amazing baby boy? What will he think? Will he eat of it when he has a choice? What if he doesn't? Will we be divided? Different? Will my eating now impact our relationship forever?"

Instead, Gen 2:6 concludes, "she took of its fruit and ate, and she also gave some to her husband who was with her and he ate." The path of selfishness is much easier to take when no one is following you. When no one close at hand is immediately affected by your decision. Would Eve have eaten the fruit and given it to Adam if she was holding her baby?

Remember, Genesis 3 starts, "Now the serpent was more crafty than any other beast of the field that the Lord God had made." Satan knew how to enter the serpent and when to tempt the humans. Get the parents to sin before they reproduce. Get their minds from God's primal command.

Postpone reproduction. Replace God's first command with another desire. Just put it off for a while.

Please, dear Christian, think about this. I will show you that, like Adam and Eve in their natural state, we have been born again to reproduce. As God wanted them to "fill the earth," so He wants, He commands us, to do the same—spiritually.

It is no small thing when we take new believers, spilling over with the joy of their salvation, and SLOW them down from their first instinct to reproduce. To share their faith. To tell someone else what Christ has done for them. And begin to teach them many other things. Good things. Maybe even biblical truths. We turn their focus from filling the earth with others born of God, to growing in their faith. To learning how to be a good member of our church or denomination. Or understanding how many books are in the Bible, or the differences between the Old and New Testaments, or the nuances of some key doctrines of the Word, etc.

When first instincts are replaced

Please don't misunderstand me. I love doctrinal truth. BUT the firstborn instinct of a born-again believer is to thank God and then share his/her faith with another. It simply cannot be otherwise. When the light of LIFE first shines on us, we MUST help others whom we love to know about it. It is instinctive. Good news simply must be shared.

We do grave and, sometimes, irreparable damage when we subtly discourage anyone from doing what we will see Christ commands all His followers to do. To take from His hand and to share His blessings with another. It was natural for Andrew to "first find his brother, Simon and tell him 'We have found the Messiah'" (John 1:41).

First things first. First commands should be first to be obeyed. God gave up His eternally loved Son for one primary purpose, "to seek and to save the lost." I hope that you are not tired of hearing that "God so loved the world, that he gave his only Son, that whoever believes in him should not perish but have eternal life" (John 3:16). That is WHY He came. Surely, many other wonderful and incredible consequences have occurred from Christ's coming. BUT, who can dare to count them as equal to the redemption of lost human souls? Jesus reasoned with multitudes saying, "For what will it profit a man if he gains the whole world and forfeits his soul? Or what shall a man give in return for his soul?" (Matthew 16:26).

What would happen if our spiritual environments nurtured new believers to immediately share their faith? Not excluding other teaching, fellowship, worship and development, but encouraging them to "go and proclaim the gospel" (Mark 16:15) alongside of growing in these other wonderful things? What would our churches be like if we all were living to reproduce and "disciple the nations?"

This question is being answered! This is happening TODAY in many locations around the world. Why not in yours? In your city, church and family? In your own life?

Why It Really Matters
Questions for Reflection (R) and ACTION (A)

1. Discuss whether this chapter resonated with you. Do you think that the parallel between the first human parents' physical reproduction and our spiritual reproduction is natural or forced? (R)

2. What was your experience when you first placed your faith in Jesus Christ? Did you want to tell someone else? Who was it and what happened? (R)

3. Did your first fire last long? If not, what happened to quench the burning flame of your witness for Christ? (R)

4. Get and begin reading Jerry Trousdale's, *Miraculous Movements*, **doing** this while you read

a. Journal everything he says about the importance and place of PRAYER in the lives of these simple, bold witnesses (A)

b. Begin to PRAY for a Disciple Making Movement to start in your area (A)

"In the gift of His Son, the revelation of His Word, the mission of His Spirit, and the institution of the Church, God has made abundant provision for the salvation of the world. That the Church has been so remiss in making known the gospel is her guilt. We must not charge the ignorance and consequent perdition of the heathen upon God. The guilt rests on us. We have kept to ourselves the bread of life and allowed the nations to perish."

-Charles Hodge (Systematic Theology vol.1) 1878

Chapter 2
Fishers of Men

In Mark's gospel, Jesus' first command to Peter and Andrew was, "Follow me and I will make you become fishers of men" (Mark 1:17). The Creator who spoke the world into existence, also spoke to His disciples. His followers. He wanted physical reproduction from Adam and Eve. And He wanted spiritual reproduction from Peter and Andrew.[1]

Called to catch others

God made the original pair, Adam and Eve, with the power to do what He commanded: *to be fruitful and to multiply*. He gave our two pair of brothers in Mark 1 the promise that He would do in and for them what they could not do for themselves. He would **make** them fishers of men. His creative power would produce in them a change. A miracle. The **FISH**ermen would be transformed into fisher**MEN**! The Creator made the first humans to reproduce and He called the first disciples to reproduce. To be involved in reproduction was not a suggestion. It was part of their responsibility as the first humans and the first disciples. They were made to reproduce.

In his lengthened account of this first call, Luke (5:1-11) portrays Jesus assuring a humbled and repentant Peter, "Do not be afraid! From now on you will catch men" (Luke 5:10b). All he had to do was to follow Jesus. Even though the command was simple, that did not make it easy. Though Jesus would do the heavy lifting, His disciples then and now have learned that much help is needed.

---

[1] All four Gospels record the call of the first disciples (Matthew 4, Mark 1, Luke 5 and John 1),

The four fishing partners who had just mightily struggled to pull in the great catch of fish, so great a haul that it had begun to tear their nets and sink their boats, would experience this life change if they surrendered, became His disciples and followed Him. If they followed, He would make them different men. Men more bent on spiritual duplication than on business success. Has Jesus called you? Has He made you a "fisher of men?"[2]

The 1st century disciples of the hundreds of Jewish rabbis in Israel knew they would someday be called on to reproduce new disciples in their rabbi's "school." I wonder, why would the four gospel writers use the same word, and call all Jesus' followers "disciples" if they did not think all would be transformed into fishers of souls? 1st century Jewish disciples were expected to reproduce. Hebrew scholar David Bivin wrote, "To make many disciples was one of the three earliest sayings recorded in the Mishnah."[3] And the Mishnah was the first authorized collection of the sayings of the ancient elders of Israel. Would Matthew, Mark, Luke and John use the word "disciple" over 200 times and mean that some of Jesus' disciples would **not** have the duty and privilege of catching others and making them disciples, too? I don't think so. All of the disciples of first century sages were expected to reproduce. Why would Jesus' disciples be different?

Yet, such is the common notion within Christianity today. You can follow Jesus and not be a disciple maker. Today, millions who call themselves "Christians" have no intention of spiritually reproducing. Many are happy going to church on Sunday and then getting on with their lives for the rest of that day and the week.

---

[2] The ESV rightly reminds us "The Greek word 'anthropoi' refers here to both men and women."
[3] Bivin, *New Light on the Difficult Words of Jesus*, 14

There is something very strange about this self-centered lifestyle, which enjoys the "Bread of life" for itself but feels little compulsion to share it with others. Yet it is common among Christians. George Barna discovered this and wrote:

"In one recent nationwide survey we asked people to describe their goals in life. Almost 9 out of 10 adults described themselves as "Christian" … But not one of the adults we interviewed said that their goal in life was to be a committed follower of Jesus Christ or to make disciples."[4]

"Intellectually, we believe that the primary reason God has blessed us is so we may enjoy life and achieve personal fulfillment. Our research has found very few Christians who, without prompting, believe that we have been blessed in order to be a blessing to others."[5]

Making Christians or disciples?

The stark difference between many 21st century Christians and the 1st century disciples of Jesus has become the focus of much of my recent research and writing. And I have concluded, with many others, that New Testament Christianity was built on the foundation of the discipleship of Jesus. Therefore, there is no authentic Christianity, today, except that which takes the terms of Christ's discipleship and carefully applies them to us.[6] If it was that "in Antioch the **disciples** were first called **Christians**" (Acts 11:26), then today—and everywhere—the same order should occur. Before someone is called a Christian, he or she should be a settled, conscientious disciple of Jesus. His Great Commission abides "to the end of the age" and its command is to "go and make disciples," not to "go and make

---

[4] Barna, *Growing True Disciples*, 7-8
[5] Barna, *Growing True Disciples*, 73
[6] For the full analysis see my *Are You a Christian or a Disciple? Rediscovering and Renewing New Testament Discipleship (2014)* and *Disciples Obey: How Christians Unknowingly Rebel against Jesus (2016)*

Christians." Any person or ministry that focuses on "making Christians" who do not understand the meaning and terms of Jesus' original call to discipleship, stands on very shaky ground. How can we know that our lives have been truly promoting His Great Commission if we do not understand what He and all His contemporaries meant by the word, "disciple"? We can't.

The initial promise to the first disciples, that if they followed Jesus, they would all become fishers of men, is a promise to all the followers of Jesus. So, each of the Gospels, the book of Acts, the letters of Paul, James, Peter and John—all include exhortations and commands to the readers which make us conclude that their writers expected everyone in the 1st century Church to be actively sharing their faith and making disciples.

To help you fully appreciate the way that all the leaders of the Early Church expected their readers to be sharing their faith with others, **please read Appendix 1—Jesus and every New Testament writer expected their readers to actively share their faith.**

If Jesus originally intended to make His disciples into fishers of men, He will do the same today with all who follow Him. Genuinely called and equipped disciples make disciples. Has this been the focus of your life and ministry? How many disciples has your ministry produced? Not how many church members? Not how many programs does your church offer? Not how many years have you been a Christian? The question is – **how many true disciples have you made?**

Why It Really Matters
Questions for Reflection (R) and ACTION (A)

1. Has your following of Jesus made you a fisher of others? Discuss the positives and negatives you have experienced down this road. (R)

2. What do you think of the quotation of Dr. Charles Hodge? (R)

3. Do you see how someone today could be a Christian without being a disciple of Christ? (R)

4. Take 3 texts quoted in Appendix 1 that most spoke to you and journal 3 people, one for each text, for whom you will begin to pray—expecting an opportunity to witness to them of Christ (A).

5. When that opportunity occurs and you bear witness, journal the results (A)

*"I am thinking today of that beautiful land
I shall reach when the sun goeth down;
When through wonderful grace by my Savior I stand,
Will there be any stars in my crown?*

(Chorus)

*"Will there be any stars, any stars in my crown,
When at evening the sun goeth down?
When I wake with the blest in the mansions of rest,
Will there be any stars in my crown?"*

*"In the strength of the Lord let me labor and pray,
Let me watch as a winner of souls;
That bright stars may be mine in the glorious day,
When His praise like the sea-billow rolls.*

*"Oh, what joy it will be when His face I behold,
Living gems at His feet to lay down;
It would sweeten my bliss in the city of gold,
Should there be any stars in my crown."*

A hymn by Eliza E Hewitt, 1897

Chapter 3

Foolish or Wise?

No one likes to be called a fool. But there are plenty of them. They have chosen to live in a very risky and dangerous way. Many Christians today think they are saved and, therefore, have eternal security—no matter what. They have been taught that if they asked Jesus into their heart, they will go to heaven. Whether they bear fruit or not. In this chapter, we will take a glimpse at two alarming Old Testament texts that might give pause to today's reckless and risky practice of assuring Christians they are heaven-bound despite their lifestyle.

> "The fruit of the righteous is a tree of life, and he who wins souls is wise" (Proverbs 11:30-NIV).

> "And many of those who sleep in the dust of the earth shall awake, some to everlasting life, and some to shame and everlasting contempt. And those who are wise shall shine like the brightness of the sky above, and those who turn many to righteousness, like the stars forever and ever" (Daniel 12:2-3)

Which way have you chosen to live?

The Book of Proverbs sets forth two great ways of life: the way of wisdom and the way of folly. Old Testament scholar, Tremper Longman explains: "Woman Wisdom is indeed a striking figure in the first nine chapters of the book, but she is not the only woman who meets the son on the path of life. Over against Woman Wisdom stands Woman Folly....

> "Proverbs 1-9 presents a picture of the ultimate encounter of the young man with these two women, whom it

purposefully compares and contrasts. The text is clear: he must choose between them....

"Proverbs 1-9 culminates in a choice that the reader must make before proceeding in the book. With whom will you dine, Woman Wisdom or Woman Folly? We now know that the choice is really between Yahweh and the false gods of the nations.

"We are left in no confusion: following Folly ... though initially inviting, results in death.... To dine with Lady Wisdom, however, brings life. She warns that ignoring her message leads to death, but obeying it brings peace: "For simpletons turn away from me—to death. Fools are destroyed by their own complacency. But all who listen to me will live in peace, untroubled by fear or harm.' (Proverbs 1:32-33)"[7]

It is in the light of these two ways that we read the Proverbs. One way leads to life and the other way, to death. The wise walk the road of wisdom and are normally saved. The foolish walk the road of folly and are often lost. In which direction are you walking?

When Jesus addressed His Jewish audience, He clearly set the scene in these same, identical terms. He said, "Everyone who hears these words of mine and does them will be like **a wise man** who builds his house on the rock.... And everyone who hears these words of mine and does not do them will be like **a foolish man** who built his house on the sand" (Matt. 7:24-27). The wise man's house stands and he remains safe through life's greatest storms. But the fool's house is destroyed—with him in it.

Let us take the two paths into the arena of spiritual reproduction. Both Proverbs 11 and Daniel 12 portray the wise

---

[7] Longman, *How to Read Proverbs*, 28-36

as being spiritually reproductive. Whereas the foolish remain fruitless and suffer for it.

Proverbs 11:30 paints the picture of a person whose life is fruitful and productive—like the original Tree of Life in the Garden of Eden. The fruit that is won or captured are other souls who are rescued and saved. "He that wins souls is wise." Soul winning is an attribute of one who walks the path of wisdom not folly. In his classic commentary on Proverbs, Charles Bridges wrote,

> "Here is the fruit of the flourishing branch (11:28). The whole course of the righteous—his influence, his prayers, his instruction, his example—is a tree of life. What the tree of life was in paradise; what it will be in heaven (Rev 22:2), that he is in this wilderness—fruitful, nourishing and healing....
>
> "This was the wisdom of our Divine Master.... And truly were these opportunities (of winning souls) 'his meat and drink.' For when 'wearied with his journey, he sat down on the well,' thirsting for water; far more intensely did he thirst for the soul of the poor sinner before him; and, having won her to himself, he forgot his own (physical need) in the joy of her salvation. (John 4:6, 32-34). In close walking after this pattern of wisdom, did the great Apostle 'become all things to all men, that he might by all means gain some' (1 Cor 9: 20-22; 10: 33). God grant that no Minister of Christ may spend a day, without laboring to win at least one soul for heaven!
>
> "But—blessed be God! —this fruit—this wisdom—is not confined to the sacred calling (of the Christian Ministry). Do we love our Lord? Arise, let us follow in this happy work, and he will honor us. The righteous wife wins her husband's soul by the wisdom of meekness and sobriety. (1 Pet 3:1-2). The godly neighbor wins his fellow sinner by the patient energy of faith and love. (James 5:19-20).

'No man' in the Church of God 'liveth unto himself.' (Rom 14:7). The Christian who neglects his brother's salvation, fearfully hazards his own."[8]

So, dare I ask you—has your life been like a fruitful tree in its spiritual reproduction? Or have you been most foolishly concerned only with your own eternal destiny?

Daniel's amazing text—one of the clearest teachings on the resurrection of the dead in all of the Old Testament—leaves us wondering the same thing. How can we expect to be part of the resurrection, of those who will shine in glory eternally, if we have not "let our lights shine before" others on earth? Who is it, according to Daniel, who will be raised to life? He clearly declares, "those who have turned many to righteousness!" Listen to the words of the amazing Matthew Henry who wrote one of the most useful commentaries on the whole Bible (1706),

> "There is a glory reserved for all the saints in the future state, for all that are wise, wise for their souls and eternity. A man's wisdom now makes his face shine (Ecc 8:1), but much more will it do so in that state where its power shall be perfected and its services rewarded. 2. The more good any do in this world, especially to the souls of men, the greater will be their glory and reward in the other world. Those that turn men to righteousness, that turn sinners from the error of their ways and help to save their souls from death (James 5:20) will share in the glory of those they have helped to heaven, which will be a great addition to their own glory."[9]

---

[8] Charles Bridges, *Exposition of the Book of Proverbs*, 129-130
[9] Matthew Henry, *Commentary on the Whole Bible, One Volume*, 1460

Is the Chinese underground church correct?

Likewise, Chinese brother Yun, called "the heavenly man," wrote,

> "Many Christians today are deceived. Somehow, they think that being saved means they can sit back and enjoy the Lord and do nothing else while they wait for Him to come again…. In China all the Christians I know are busy working for the Lord, preaching the gospel to people nearby and to those far away…doing all they can to advance the kingdom of God. In China every believer is an evangelist…. They want to be like one of those mentioned in the Bible, which declares, 'Those who are wise will shine like the brightness of the heavens, and those who lead many to righteousness, like the stars for ever and ever.' (Dan. 12:3)."[10]

When one is in an African Game Park and spots one of the "Big Five," it is customary to stop the car and share the location with other tourists. Many people have never seen a leopard. I can hardly describe the joy in sharing the location of a leopard with others. No one thinks you are rude when you wave them down and share "the good news." They are so thankful and hurry off to see the treasured animal themselves.

How "good" is the Good News of the Gospel to you if you have not urgently and effectively shared it with someone else? Believe me, it is no excuse for you to say, "No one that I know is seeking. No one is longing." Jesus trained His disciples how to go and find the people whom He is preparing to become disciples. He has taught us HOW to access these "people of peace." If you are really interested in being a disciple who makes disciples, the testimonies and books explaining HOW

---

[10] Paul Hattaway and Brother Yun, Living Water, 232

are at your fingertips.[11] Take some time to read Appendix 2: Evangelism-then and now, if you really want to know the difference between our largely ineffective western evangelistic methods and the way that today is seeing the most ordinary disciples yielding the most amazing fruitfulness.

Why It Really Matters
Questions for Reflection (R) and ACTION (A)

1. How may those who are still "foolish" be comfortable while attending a Christian church today? (R)

2. When you compare the way of wisdom portrayed by Proverbs 11:30, how does your life stack up? (R)

3. Does Daniel 12:2-3 bless or worry you? (R)

4. Discuss the difference between the Chinese Christians described by Brother Yun and those whom you know. (R)

5. Journal Jesus' commands in Luke 10:1-12 and write down 5 possible "people of peace" (A)

---

[11] See Jerry Trousdale's, Miraculous Movements; David Watson's, Contagious Disciple Making; Jim Lily's, Great Commission Disciple Making, Ralph Moore's, Making Disciples, Juan Carlos Ortiz's, Disciple

"Must I go, and empty-handed,
Thus my dear Redeemer meet?
Not one day of service give Him,
Lay no trophy at His feet?

Refrain:

"Must I go, and empty-handed?"
Must I meet my Savior so?
Not one soul with which to greet Him,
Must I empty-handed go?"

Not at death I shrink or falter,
For my Savior saves me now;
But to meet Him empty-handed,
Thought of that now clouds my brow.

Oh, the years in sinning wasted,
Could I but recall them now,
I would give them to my Savior,
To His will I'd gladly bow.

Oh, ye saints, arouse, be earnest,
Up and work while yet 'tis day;
Ere the night of death o'ertake thee,
Strive for souls while still you may."

A hymn by Charles C Luther, 1877

Chapter 4
Good and Faithful Servant?

In the last week of His life, during what many call "Passion Week," Jesus went daily into the temple and spoke to the pilgrims attending the festival of Passover. Many of the kingdom parables he told had a similar message. Be ready for the Lord's return. Be watching and working for Him as you wait His return. The Son of God repeatedly warned His servants about getting distracted, comfortable, or sinking their roots down too deeply into this world. Especially if the Lord delays His return. Read the following message of Jesus carefully:

> "For it will be like a man going on a journey, who called his servants and entrusted to them his property. To one he gave five talents, to another two, to another one, each according to his ability. Then he went away. He who had received five talents went at once and traded with them, and he made five talents more. So, also he who had the two talents made two talents more. But he who had received the one talent went and dug in the ground and hid his master's money.
>
> Now after a long time the master of those servants came and settled accounts with them. And he who had received the five talents came forward, bringing five talents more, saying, 'Master, you delivered to me five talents here I have made five talents more.' His master said to him, 'Well done, good and faithful servant. You have been faithful over a little; I will set you over much. Enter into the joy of your master.
>
> And he also who had the two talents came forward, saying, 'Master you delivered to me two talents; here I have made two talents more.' His master said to him, 'Well done,

good and faithful servant. You have been faithful over a little, I will set you over much. Enter into the joy of your master.'

He also who had received the one talent came forward, saying, 'Master, I knew you to be a hard man, reaping where you did not sow, and gathering where you scattered no seed, so I was afraid, and I went and hid your talent in the ground. Here you have what is yours. But the master answered him, 'You wicked and slothful servant! You knew that I reap where I have not sown and gather where I scattered no seed? Then you ought to have invested my money with the bankers, and at my coming I should also receive what was my own with interest. So take the talent from him and give it to him who has the ten talents. For to everyone who has will more be given, and he will have an abundance. But from the one who has not, even what he has will be taken away. And cast the worthless servant into the outer darkness. In that place will be weeping and gnashing of teeth" (Matthew 25:14-30)[12]

I understand the art of interpreting parables. I am not going to push this parable beyond its obvious points. I don't have to. The main message is obvious. The servants of Christ had better be taking all He has given us and be using it wisely, looking for making "capital gains." All we have is His not ours. We are His bondservants or slaves. And what we have been given is all to be used wisely in the advancement of His Kingdom. These parables of the Kingdom reveal the nature of God's Kingdom. And this parable speaks of those servants who will be welcomed to enter His Kingdom and those who will not be thus welcomed. A more solemn teaching could hardly be

---

[12] Several of Jesus' last week actions and messages focused on fruitfulness. Consider His warnings in the others, just as we have focused on this one: Jesus Curses the Unfruitful Fig Tree (Matt. 21:18-22), The Parable of the Two Sons (Matt. 21:28-32), and The Parable of the Tenants (Matthew 21:33-46).

considered by those who consider themselves Christ's children, His servants, His Bride. This parable separates some servants of Christ from other servants. Some will be received and others will be rejected. This is serious stuff because none of us are expecting to be rejected.

What if this teaching means exactly what it obviously says in all of its naked clarity? Many are hoping that it does not. They are taking a dreadful gamble. What if Jesus is here teaching that true, saving faith must be productive? That real faith multiplies? And that multiplying two times, or producing 100% gain is "very little?" Does your Savior deserve little or nothing from you? Have you multiplied your faith for your Lord?

A grace that demands nothing?

Many of us have fallen asleep to such warnings. We have embraced a theology that has so much perverted grace in it, we are demanded to do nothing for the One who did everything for us. The Lutheran church in Hitler's time had largely fallen asleep, trusting in a defiled type of grace. One of its fiercest critics, the German Lutheran, Dietrich Bonhoeffer wrote, "Cheap grace is the deadly enemy of our Church. We are fighting today for costly grace."[13] With Bonhoeffer and many others, I am saying that true faith works. True faith is active. And one of its indispensable characteristics is that one who possesses true faith must share it. Not perfectly. Not constantly. But, the thrust and theme of this book and the hymns, quotes and verses it contains is simply this: If you do not witness and spread the Gospel, if you do not multiply spiritually—you likely are not saved.

Listen to the further warnings of Bonhoeffer, especially if you have found in your understanding of "the grace of God," a loophole for spiritual laziness and unproductivity.

---

[13] Dietrich Bonhoeffer, *The Cost of Discipleship*, 45

"Cheap grace is grace without discipleship, grace without the cross, without Jesus Christ, living and incarnate.... Costly grace is the treasure hidden in the field; for the sake of it a man will gladly go and sell all that he has. It is the pearl of great price.... It is the kingly rule of Christ, for whose sake a man will pluck out the eye which causes him to stumble; it is the call of Jesus Christ at which the disciple leaves his nets and follows him.... Such grace is **costly** because it calls us to follow, and it is **grace** because it calls us to follow Jesus Christ. It is **costly** because it costs a man his life, and it is **grace** because it gives a man the only true life."[14]

A missionary voice from long ago

The Christian voices are so few today that speak this truth that we often need to go to other decades and centuries in World Christian History to hear it spoken with force and clarity. Listen to a missionary who went to the Pacific islands in a day when "going" meant almost certain death. I have chosen just ten quotes taken from a powerful book of 225 pages that was published after its author had died spreading the gospel:

> 1. To be faithful stewards, then, we must fully occupy for God all the talents in our possession.... With this understanding, there must be no reserve. Reserve is robbery. (33)

> 2. Can we be faithful stewards, and not contrive, study and devise the best ways of using the talents that God has entrusted to us, so that they may turn to the greatest account in his service? Is not the glory of God and the eternal salvation of our ruined race, an object worthy of as much determination of purpose as a little

---

[14] Bonhoeffer, 47

property which must soon be wrapped in flames...? (35)

3. Is it not a fact that will strike us dumb..., that it is the love of money, and not zeal for God, that digs canals, lays railroads, runs steamboats...and is, in short, the main spring of every undertaking? The love of money has explored the land and seas...? (38)

4. Things deemed comfortable and convenient may be multiplied without limit—consume all of God's wealth and leave the world in ruins. If the world were not in ruins, then it might be proper to seek not only the comforts, but even the elegancies of life. (41)

5. The disposition to go everywhere, regardless of wealth, and with Jesus on our lips, must be the spirit of the church.... (53)

6. The heathen world, as a mass, has been left to perish. And by whom? Not by the Father of mercies--he gave his Son to redeem it. Not by the Savior of sinners--look at Calvary. Not by the Holy Spirit—his influences have been ever ready. Not by the angels—their wings have never tired when sent on errands of mercy. All that Heaven could do has been done, consistently with the all-wise arrangement of committing an important agency to the church. The church has been slothful and negligent. Each generation of Christians has in turn received the vast responsibility, neglected it in a great measure, and transmitted it to the next. The guilt of this neglect who can estimate? (61)

7. (We) have little conception in what is meant by total consecration to God. There must be an entire reform in this matter. Every Christian must feel that his employment, whether it be agriculture, merchandise, medicine, law, or anything else, is of no value any farther than it is connected with the Redeemer's

kingdom; that wealth is trash, and life a trifle, except as they may be used to advance the cause of Christ; and that as far as they may be used for this purpose, they are of immense value. Let every Christian feel this sentiment—let it be deeply engraved on his heart, and how long, think you, would financial means be lacking in the work of the world's salvation? (81)

8. There is no cheap or easy way of converting the world. (191)

9. Remember the time is short.... Keep in mind the conduct of our blessed Savior, and be imbued with his spirit. Feel as he felt, and do as he did, when he beheld us in our misery and sin. (196)

10. At the judgment day, if I mistake not, we will see a great deal of our conduct in a different light than we do now. (224)[15]

Current voices from China

These words, written about 175 years ago, powerfully address the temptation that has always confronted Christians, especially in times of freedom and affluence. But, even in our day, there are some voices boldly declaring our duty and privilege to be Christ's fruitful witnesses. Even when it costs us physical torture and other deprivations. Some of the leaders of the Chinese house church movement, estimated to exceed 100 million believers, have declared:

> "Prior to the 1950s, most Christians in China were also mere 'believers' in Christ, and when the heat of affliction came on, many fell away from the faith. Many others, however, got serious about God and decided to follow him whatever the cost. They were gradually

---

[15] Sheldon Dibble, Thoughts on Missions, 33-224

transformed into disciples of the Lord Jesus Christ, who not only preached Jesus on the cross but realized that there is also a personal cross on which each disciple will experience crucifixion and pain.

"Today most Christians in China's house churches are fully committed disciples of Jesus Christ. Every Christian is a soul-winner; every believer is involved in fulfilling the Great Commission."[16]

I know that many Christians expect they will hear, "Well done, good and faithful servant" when they stand before the Lord. It goes without saying that the true definition of "good and faithful" is critical. If the current Chinese house church disciples are correct, if you are not reproducing, you have been neither good nor faithful.

Of course, I agree here with our Chinese brothers. Please understand that I really do trust the gospel and abhor legalism. But emphasizing the commands of Jesus regarding bearing fruit does not necessarily lead to self-righteousness. My friend, Roy Moran, reminds us, "Legalism is holding people accountable to human laws. Jesus was not asking us to obey any rules or guidelines laid down by humans.... Obeying Jesus leads to freedom not legalism."[17] These Chinese Brothers and old missionary Dibble well portray truly free followers of Jesus. Holy Spirit remind us of just how good the Good News is! And help us become free from fear and self-consciousness so we can speak to others daily about Christ! Help us to be privileged to hear, "Well done, good and faithful servant" when we stand before the Master of the Universe, Jesus Christ!

---

[16] Brother Yun, Peter Xu and Enoch Wang in *Back to Jerusalem*, 115
[17] Roy Moran, Spent Matches, 37

Why It Really Matters
Questions for Reflection (R) and ACTION (A)

1. Does Charles Luther's hymn strike you as dealing with a good question or as unnecessary concerns? (R)

2. What is your plan to ensure that you will be greeted with, "Well done!" from Christ? (R)

3. In the Parable of the 10 Minas (Luke 19:11-27), the nobleman commanded his servants to "occupy until I come" (19:13-NKJV). The ESV reads, "Engage in business until I come." If this represents the orders of Jesus to us, what is our business until He comes? What do you think should occupy your time? (R)

4. Do something sacrificial or costly to you this week that will advance Christ's Kingdom (A)

5. Journal the result of that and share the praise with another (A)

"There is a fatal defect in the life of Christ's church in the 20th century: a lack of true discipleship. Discipleship means forsaking everything to follow Christ. But for many of today's supposed Christians—perhaps the majority—it is the case that while there is much talk about Christ and even furious activity, there is actually very little following Christ Himself. And that means in some circles there is very little genuine Christianity. Many who fervently call him 'Lord, Lord' are not Christians."

Dr James M. Boice (Christ's Call to Discipleship) 1986

"Very likely your religion costs you nothing. Very probably it neither costs you trouble, nor time, nor thought, nor care, nor pains, nor reading, nor praying, nor self-denial, nor conflict, nor working, nor labor of any kind…. Such a religion as this will never save your soul…A religion which costs nothing is worth nothing."

Bishop J.C. Ryle (1816-1900)

Chapter 5

Who is on God's Side?

Usually great things are accomplished over a long time. But when we read the four Gospels, the vast amount of the material deals with only 3.5 years of Jesus' young adult life. The experiences and truth that flowed from those relatively few months in His life have had a greater impact on the world than all the writings of all philosophers of all ages! Today we marvel at the endless lessons and grace we derive from these few years of the life of Christ. Those who followed Him found in Him much more than they had ever dreamed. But it was not all thrills and chills. There were frequent times of testing and tears, too.

The context

Jesus' first ministry year was one of great popularity, followed by growing months of opposition and accusation. These times culminated in a dreadful showdown with the Sanhedrin, the religious leaders of the Jewish people. He lived and taught spectacularly and, then, died horrifically. Following Jesus was not an easy thing to do.

The growing tension during that window of time is recorded throughout the Gospels. A little background of that fateful moment in human history should prove helpful. The first 70 years of the 1st century was a time of great messianic expectation among the Jewish people and many of their leaders. So it was a time when signs or miracles were anticipated. Most Jewish leaders believed in miracles. And they were convinced that there were some miracles which only the coming Messiah would be able to do. The Hebrew expert, Joseph Amaral, recently wrote a book that deals in length with the Coming Messiah and His miracles. He states,

"Jesus performed so many miracles, but why did the Pharisees react more to some than others? This is a valid question to which there is a reasonable answer. Sometime prior to the coming of Jesus, the rabbis divided miracles into two separate categories—those that anyone could perform if empowered to do so by God and those reserved only for the Messiah....

"Every time there was a possible candidate for the Messiah, it was standard procedure to dispatch a group of Pharisees to interview the person and check him out....

"Every time a Messianic miracle was accomplished, the Pharisees immediately went to investigate.... Invariably they would be disappointed, because that candidate would only perform one of the four necessary miracles required to be the Messiah. Then Jesus of Nazareth appeared on the scene. He didn't just perform one Messianic miracle, or two, or three, but He performed all four...miracles—healing a leper, casting out a mute demon, healing a man born blind, and raising someone from the dead after four days."[18]

The contest

Not surprisingly, the Gospel accounts reveal Jesus' performing all four of these "messianic miracles." Healing multiple lepers (Luke 10:11-19), a man born blind (John 9:1-7) and Lazarus, after he had been dead for four days (John 11:38-44). The growing frustration of the investigating Jewish leaders may be seen in most of the accounts.

But the volcano erupts after Jesus heals a blind mute whose condition had been caused by an oppressing demon. The

---

[18] Joseph Amaral in *Understanding Jesus*, 7-9

people in amazement were asking, "Can this be the Son of David?" But "when the Pharisees heard it they said, 'It is only by Beelzebul, the prince of demons, that this man casts out demons." (Matt. 12:24). Jesus replied with a clear declaration of who was on His side and by issuing a severe warning:

> "If I cast out demons by Beelzebul, by whom do your sons cast them out? Therefore, they will be your judges. But if it is by the Spirit of God that I cast out demons, then the kingdom of God has come upon you. Or how can someone enter a strong man's house and plunder his goods unless he first binds the strong man? Then indeed he may plunder his house. Whoever is not with me is against me, and whoever does not gather with me scatters. Therefore, I tell you, every sin and blasphemy will be forgiven people, but the blasphemy against the Spirit will not be forgiven.... Either make the tree good and its fruit good, or make the tree bad and its fruit bad, for the tree is known by its fruit.... I tell you, on the day of judgement people will give account for every careless word they speak, for by your words you will be justified and by your words you will be condemned." (Matt 12:27-36)

The conclusion

So, the people had come to an absolute fork in the road. Most of their leaders had determined that Jesus was demonized beyond any man—by the very power of Satan, himself! And Jesus claimed precisely the opposite as this colossal contest that would determine the destiny of both humans and nations was playing out before their eyes 2000 years ago.

I am amazed that when most Christians read this account they come away with a single concern. What is the unpardonable sin? We are both frightened and fascinated by an unforgiveable sin, so a good deal of attention is paid to that subject. But was Jesus saying that the main issue before the people was whether or not they blasphemed the Holy Spirit? Did Jesus answer the great question— "Who is on God's side—Jesus or the Pharisees?" simply affirming--those who do not blaspheme the Spirit are on God's side?

No, He did not. Jesus warned them of not recognizing and denouncing the work of the Spirit. But, tucked away in this story—almost out of sight—is the answer for which the Jewish multitudes were longing. And its statement still stands for those Christians today who might be wondering—How can we tell which group is really best representing God?

Here is the answer to the question that plagued them and millions today. And, remember, when Jesus said the following, it was God who spoke!

> *"Whoever is not with me is against me, and whoever does not gather with me scatters"* (Matt 12:30).

In other words, those who choose to be my disciples, alone, are on safe ground. Disciples followed their rabbis. They were "with" their sage constantly. Before any were called Christians, believers in Acts were called "disciples" (Acts 11:26). For the undeniable marks of a 1st century disciple, see my previous books.[19] Are you on God's side? Well, if you do not follow Jesus like a disciple, you are against Jesus. That is the clear meaning of these words, which were spoken when the stakes could not have been greater.

As He did then, so now Jesus invites all to follow Him as disciples. Both men and women. "Come to me, all who labor and are heavy laden, and I will give you rest. Take my yoke upon you, and learn from me, for I am gentle and lowly in heart, and you will find rest for your souls. For my yoke is easy and my burden is light." (Matt 11:28-30). Life-long scholar of the Jewish background of the Gospels, David Bivin, wrote,

---

[19] Edward N Gross, *Are You a Christian or a Disciple?* 39-47, 175-287; *Disciples Obey*, 25-40

"How would Jesus' first listeners have heard his words about taking on his yoke? Learning what a 'yoke' meant in the writings and culture of Jesus' time will greatly clarify his words. In a rabbi-disciple relationship, the disciple was expected to place himself in a position of total obedience and dedication to his rabbi and his philosophy. It was his desire to become just like him. This was said to be taking on the 'yoke' of the rabbi."[20]

When Jesus said, "Whoever is not **with me** is against me," He was saying, whoever does not follow Me as a disciple is against me. It was as if He said, "Whoever keeps a safe distance from Me in this great contest of light and darkness has chosen darkness." You see, to be a "church going Christian" today may not be safe at all. There are many Christians who are not disciples. They have no desire or devotion to follow Christ throughout the day everywhere they go.

Christ's second statement builds on His first, "And whoever does not gather **with me** scatters." You probably did not know that every disciple looked forward to the day when the rabbi sanctioned him to go and make other disciples. Every disciple was a disciple maker. The number of rabbis with disciples numbered in the hundreds in Jesus' day. Everyone understood that "gathering with a rabbi" meant duplicating and making other disciples. Just as Jesus lived to gather precious souls, so would His disciples.

The challenge

So, as we conclude, some difficult questions need to be asked. How many souls have you gathered? How many disciples have you made? You cannot excuse yourself by saying, "It is not my gift." Being a disciple is not a spiritual gift possessed only by a

---

[20] David Bivin, *New Light on the Difficult Words of Jesus*, 23; see also Ben Sira 51:23-27; 6:23-31

few. Discipleship is the form of relationship which Jesus and His apostles equated with true salvation! If you are not a gathering disciple—you are a scatterer. You must understand that to do no harvesting, results in scattering. The harvest remains spoiled, unpicked in the field. Many Christians are busy working, but their work is not harvest-related. Jesus wanted them and us to know that focusing on the wrong thing may also scatter. Certainly, to disobey or not to fulfill the Great Commission is "to scatter."

Who is on God's side in the great battle of life? Jesus answers, (1) those who follow, walk with, submit to Him- becoming His disciples and (2) no one is a disciple who refuses to gather, to harvest with Christ.

The words of Jesus could hardly have been any clearer than this: "Whoever is not with me is against me, and whoever does not gather with me scatters." Whoever means you and me. May we surrender to Him and seek the filling of His Holy Spirit so that we will be empowered to effectively gather with Him.

Why it Really Matters
Questions for Reflection (R) and ACTION (A)

1. Think about just how blind humans can be. Even religious, devout, biblically literate leaders! (R)

2. Does your life reveal one who is "with" Jesus more than being "apart" from Him? (R)

3. Think about how a passive Christian life does more harm than good—how we can scatter when we are not actively involved in gathering souls for the Kingdom. (R)

4. Invite another person to begin praying with you for a DMM (A)

5. Invite a non-believing friend who might be a person of peace to do something together that will deepen your friendship (A)

"Reproduction through discipling is the pattern of the evangelistic explosion all through the Acts. Though attention centers upon a few leading spirits who are setting the pace, the real work of multiplication comes through the steady, unpretentious, faithful witness of the brethren."

Robert Coleman (The Master Plan of Discipleship) 1987

Chapter 6
When filled with the Spirit you will ...

The book of Acts gives a very focused and brief history of the Church from the time of Jesus' resurrection in Jerusalem to the time of Paul's house arrest in Rome, Italy. This history spanned some 35 years. Its author, Luke, was one of the Apostle Paul's missionary companions. He saw with his own eyes the transformation that occurred when the Holy Spirit filled a disciple of Jesus. And he credited the great progress of the Church throughout the Mediterranean world to the powerful work of the Spirit of God. He makes it crystal clear from both his Gospel and the book of Acts that without the Holy Spirit's empowering presence, the Church is sunk.

So, after giving the Great Commission to His Apostles, commanding them that "repentance and forgiveness of sins should be proclaimed in his name to all nations beginning at Jerusalem" (Lk 24:47), Luke has Jesus concluding His words on earth with these: "And behold, I am sending the promise of my Father upon you. But stay in the city until you are clothed with power from on high" (Luke 24:49). And then He ascends, blessing them, into heaven.

He commissioned them to go, but not until they were empowered with the Holy Spirit. How thoroughly He had prepared them! He had shown them the way to make disciples and sent them out on short mission trips to practice the art. He had prayed with and for them. He had spoken to them for 40 days following His resurrection (Acts 1:3); but Jesus concluded with this promise: "you will receive power when the Holy Spirit has come upon you, and you shall be my witnesses in Jerusalem and in all Judea and Samaria, and to the ends of the earth" (Acts 1:8).

The training of Jesus was not enough!

As great as the training had been for the apostles, they needed something more. Something substantially different than the experiences that the Savior had given them. They needed to be owned, filled and fueled with the Spirit of the Living God! For this they had to wait. And they did wait prayerfully until, after ten days, Jesus baptized them with the Holy Spirit. On Pentecost, after the Spirit descended in power on them, Peter declared, "This Jesus God raised up, and of that we are all witnesses. Being therefore exalted at the right hand of God, and having received from the father the promise of the Holy Spirit, he has poured out this that you yourselves are seeing and hearing" (Acts 2:32-33). What John the Baptist had promised was then and there fulfilled, "He will baptize you with the Holy Spirit and with fire" (Matt 3:11). The Early Church of 120 experienced true revival. They were already saved. But now they were specially enabled by the reviving Spirit of God.

After this Pentecostal revival they would be filled with the Spirit many times. Luke hardly tires of describing those moments in the life of these early disciples. He mentions the Spirit of God some 60 times in Acts. And Luke portrays Him "filling believers" nine different times in Acts.[21] The simple fact is this, there is one and only one common effect that the coming of the Spirit had on those disciples. **When they were filled, they spoke**. They shared their faith, the Word of God, the praises of God, even three times speaking messages in new languages. The verbal effect of the Spirit's filling was expressed in numerous ways. But one thing was constant—they opened their mouths and bore witness of Jesus Christ.

Acts 4:31 is representative when it reveals, "And when they had prayed the place in which they were gathered was shaken, and they were all filled with the Holy Spirit and continued to

---

[21] See Acts 2:4,11,16-17; 4:8; 4:23-31; 6:3,5,7,10; 9:17,20; 10:44-48; 11:22-24; 13:4-12; 19:6

speak the word of God with boldness." To Luke, and thus to Paul, when one is Spirit-controlled, he or she will impact others with what they say.

We do not fill our cars to keep them parked in the garage. And God does not fill us with the Holy Spirit to remain where we were. To stand speechless. But to declare the good news of the Great King and His Kingdom.

Do you have the Spirit of God?

The Early Church was a quickly growing church. Dynamic. On the move. Or as Jesus commanded, "Going...make disciples." They certainly were not at a standstill. Deadlocked. Paul likened the filling of the Spirit with inebriation. He wrote, "And do not get drunk with wine, for that is debauchery, but be filled with the Spirit" (Ephesians 5:18). When the 120 were filled or baptized with the Spirit on Pentecost, some onlookers mocked saying, "they are filled with new wine" (Acts 2:13). When people get drunk, they "loosen up." The shy begin to speak freely. The small and weak man is no longer intimidated, but takes a swing at the muscularly built man standing in front of him. Usually he doesn't connect—but it is not for lack of trying. He is bold. Some would say, he is out of his mind.

But, you see, that is the point, isn't it? When we are filled with the Spirit of God we dare to say and do what otherwise we would not. We are brave, courageous, even fearless. We are "not ourselves." At such a time we surprise people and sometimes offend them. But be sure of this—we speak.

When the young missionary Saul of Tarsus was first called "Paul," it was when, "Paul, filled with the Holy Spirit, looked intently at him and said, 'You son of the devil, you enemy of all righteousness, full of all deceit and villainy, will you not stop making crooked the straight paths of the Lord?'" (Acts 13:9-10). The demonic Elymas was immediately blinded by God and the governor of the island of Crete "believed, when he saw what had occurred, for he was astonished at the teaching of the Lord" (Acts 13:12). It is not always predictable what will be said when one is filled with the Spirit. But this much is certain—something will be spoken.

So, please do not miss my point. If you say you saved, you are claiming to have the Spirit of God. Paul unequivocally states, "Anyone who does not have the Spirit of Christ, does not belong to him" (Romans 8:9). So here is the question, how often does the Spirit lead you to speak about Jesus?

What Jesus said would happen to everyone who believes

The apostle John recorded,

> "...Jesus stood up and cried out...'Whoever believes in me, as the Scripture has said, 'Out of his heart will flow rivers of living water.' Now this he said about the Spirit, whom those who believed in him were to receive, for as yet the Spirit had not been given, because Jesus was not yet glorified" (John 7:38-39).

The fulfillment of this promise is seen throughout the book of Acts in the life of the Early Church. Why is this not true today among so many Christians? Why is there barely a trickle, when Jesus said there would be rivers flowing from the hearts of those who believe?

Here's an answer, coming from Spirit-filled Peter who could then boldly speak to the Jewish leaders when just weeks prior he had no courage and denied Jesus three times,

> "And we are witnesses to these things, and so is the Holy Spirit, whom God has given to those who obey him" (Acts 5:32).

Did you get that? There is a special empowering of the Spirit that comes to those who OBEY God. If you do NOT obey Christ's command, "go and make disciples," His command to "let your light shine before others," Paul's command to "let your speech always be gracious, seasoned with salt, so that you may know how to answer each person"[22]—then you are grieving the Holy Spirit and His power will not flow in and through you. You must want the living water to flow through you. Let it flow!

At the end of all Sacred Scripture, John wrote, "The Spirit and the Bride say, 'Come.'" That is what the Spirit will always lead the Bride to express when He fills us. "Let the one who is thirsty come; let the one who desires take the water of life without price" (Rev 22:17).

"You will receive power when the Holy Spirit has come upon you, and you will be my witnesses…to the ends of the earth" (Acts 1:8). When you are filled, you will speak. And when you speak, you will bear fruit. My conclusion to this chapter on the Holy Spirit's role as the One who empowers witness is these words by "the heavenly man," Brother Yun:

> "Now let me ask you something personal. Do you have streams of living water flowing from your life? Do you experience the joy of the Lord, or has your Christian life become dry and dusty, based on human intellect and empty rituals? Before you will ever experience God's living water, you will need to be immersed in it yourself.
>
> "If you have never experienced God's living water inside of you, then I encourage you to fall to your knees, cry out to God, and repent of your sins. Ask Him to change your life, and dedicate the rest of your days to serving God and not yourself.
>
> "If you do know God but it has been years since you felt that fresh presence of the Lord Jesus Christ in your life, then you too should fall on your knees and seek God.… To all who believe in His Son, God gives His grace and

---

[22] Matthew 28:19; Matthew 5:16; Colossians 4:5-6

provides living water to flow from within you, bringing life to every area of your life that has been unfruitful and broken."[23]

So, your surrender to the filling and the empowering of the Spirit is essential to continue down the path of following Jesus and being His bold witnesses. Your surrender must be willing and not coerced. A God of love will be loved by those who serve Him. Do you love Him as One always near you? Is Jesus a powerfully present Companion and Leader to you daily?[24] This is what the Spirit does within you—He enables you to follow Jesus. "When the Spirit of truth comes, He will glorify me" (John 16:13-14). The Spirit within you, fills you to follow Jesus who is with you. The Spirit will remind you of the presence of Jesus, who promised, "I am with you always, to the end of the age." (See Appendix 3- No GOING without being SENT).

Why it Really Matters
Questions for Reflection (R) and ACTION (A)

1. Has your Christian life depended on the daily filling of the Spirit? (R)

2. Meditate on and memorize Acts 1:8—then begin to surrender daily to Jesus, seeking the filling of the Spirit and the courageous witness that He, alone, gives. (A)

---

[23] Brother Yun, *Living Water*, 128-129
[24] See my *Disciples Obey* chapter 5, Christ's Presence Obedience, pp 116-135

3. Please ponder the closing words of the severely persecuted and amazingly fruitful Brother Yun, our contemporary, and repent of whatever sin the Spirit convicts you of. (R & A)

"Go, labor on; spend, and be spent;
Thy joy to do the Father's will;
It is the way the Master went;
Should not the servant tread it still?

"Go, labor on: 'tis not for naught;
Thy earthly loss is heav'nly gain;
Men heed thee, love thee, praise thee not;
The Master praises, what are men?

"Go, labor on; your hands are weak,
Your knees are faint, your souls cast down;
Yet falter not; the prize you seek
Is near, a kingdom and a crown.

"Go, labor on while it is day,
The world's dark night is hastening on;
Speed, speed thy work, cast sloth away,
It is not thus that souls are won.

"Men die in darkness at your side,
Without a hope to cheer the tomb;
Take up the torch and wave it wide,
The torch that lights time's thickest gloom.

"Press on, faint not, keep watch and pray;
Be wise the erring soul to win;
Go forth into the world's highway,
Compel the wanderer to come in.

"Press on, and in thy work rejoice;
For work comes rest, the prize thus won;
Soon shalt thou hear the Master's voice,
The midnight cry, Behold, I come!"

A hymn by Horatio Bonar (1808-1889)

Chapter 7
I Looked for Fruit

In this chapter I want to ask you to do one thing: If possible, please try to put yourself in God's place. If you carefully read the following Old Testament texts, you will see why our unchanging Creator and Redeemer cannot look approvingly on the state of fruitlessness that many churches and Christians exhibit today.

A dear pastor friend of mine recently made this observation. We all want to claim the **promises** God made to Israel in the Old Testament; but no one believes we might be heirs to their **problems**, too! We want the blessings, but do not think we might be guilty of the backslidings! Is it possible that large parts of the church in the West are actually showing the same reluctance to obey God that marked large sections of the history of Israel? Could it be that, like the multitudes who marveled at the ministry of Jesus, many Christians today "seeing, do not see, and hearing, they do not hear, nor do they understand" (Matthew 13:13)? Read what God said about fruitfulness in these Old Testament passages and ask yourselves: Is that true of me? Does that describe my friends and my church?

What more could I have done?

> "Let me sing for my beloved my love song concerning his vineyard: My beloved had a vineyard on a very fertile hill. He dug it and cleared it of stones, and planted it with choice vines; he built a watchtower amid it, and hewed out a wine vat in it; and **he looked for it to yield grapes**, but it yielded wild grapes.
>
> "And now, O inhabitants of Jerusalem and men of Judah, judge between me and my vineyard. **What more was**

there to do for my vineyard, that I have not done in it? When I looked for it to yield grapes, why did it yield wild grapes?

"And now I will tell you what I will do to my vineyard. I will remove its hedge, and it shall be devoured; I will break down its wall, and it shall be trampled down. I will make it a waste; and it shall not be pruned or hoed, and briers and thorns shall grow up; I will also command the clouds that they rain no rain upon it.

"For the vineyard of the Lord of hosts is the house of Israel, and the men of Judah are his pleasant planting; and he looked for justice, but behold bloodshed; for righteousness, but behold an outcry! (Isaiah 5:1-7).

Aren't you yet convinced that the theme of this book is true? That God expects His children to reproduce? Do you not believe that God is looking for fruit from you? And what are you producing? Succulent, ravishing, reproductive grapes or wild grapes? Grapes that are bitter and useless?

Let me ask you: what more could God have done for YOU than what He has done to make you fruitful? Beyond Israel, dear Christian, He has provided for you:

-the Messiah, Jesus of Nazareth

-Who died for your sins

-Who was raised for your justification

-Who, with the Father, poured out the Holy Spirit, making your body His temple

-Who gave you 27 inspired New Testament books beyond the 39 Old Testament books

-Who has proven Himself throughout World Christian History to be the Savior and Leader of all who will follow Him

-Who has called you, given to you the gift of repentance, offered you full and free forgiveness through His own mist precious blood

-Who has united you to a living community of faith to encourage you and pray with you

-And Who will come again, rewarding all who follow Him by faith and punishing all who reject Him, who do not obey Him, who do not serve Him as Lord and King.

What more could God have done for you?

And what does He command of you? To follow Him. To speak of Him by the power of the Holy Spirit to those whom He prepares and brings into your lives. He expects you to confess Him before others. What He has given to you, He has commanded you to freely give to others.

Yes, Jesus expects you to keep His commands as a proof that you truly love Him. Remember, it says **in the Great Commission**, "teach them to obey everything that I have commanded you" (Matt 28:20 – NIV). Are you obeying the command of the Great Commission? Are you making obedient, reproducing disciples?

Perhaps you think that there is no way that God will judge you. That, because of His grace, you have nothing to fear—even though your life is totally or virtually fruitless. Read carefully Appendix 5 and the following **New Testament** words written to church-gathering Christians:

> "Therefore, we must pay much closer attention to what we have heard, lest we drift away from it. For since the message declared by angels (in the Old Testament) proved to be reliable, and every transgression or disobedience received a just retribution, **how shall we escape if we neglect such a great a salvation?**" (Hebrews 2:1-3a)

No, you cannot claim the blessings of the Old Testament people of God, without understanding that you, like them, can drift away. That you can grow cold and selfish and comfortable. That you can forget "to work out your own salvation with fear and trembling." (Philippians 2:12b).

Read how Israel grew away from their God, abusing their prosperity and blessings:

Fruitful for whom?

> "Israel is a luxuriant vine that yields its fruit. The more his fruit increased, the more altars he built; as his country improved, he improved his pillars. Their heart is false; now they must bear their guilt. The Lord will break down their altars and destroy their pillars.... Sow for yourselves righteousness; reap steadfast love; break up your fallow ground, for it is time to seek the Lord, that he may come and rain righteousness upon you. (Hosea 10:1, 12)

There are numerous books recently written that have warned American Evangelicals of the serious state of membership decline our churches are presently in, even while some other outward conditions might be improving.[25] We can be "growing" without God raining righteousness upon us. It is time to repent, to break up those hardened clods, to become fruitful.

Read how prosperity and possessions, the good life, can create a spirit of apathy and unproductivity.

---

[25] See Dickerson, John S - *The Great Evangelical Recession – 6 Factors that will crash the American Church and how to prepare;* Kinnaman, David - *You Lost Me;* Julia Duin, *Quitting Church;* David T Olson, *The American Church in Crisis;* Christine Wicker, *The Fall of the Evangelical Nation; Drew* Dyck, *Generation Ex-Christian,* Josh McDowell, *The Last Christian Generation,* George Barna, *Revolution;* Barna, *Futurecast.*

Lazy or fruitful?

"I passed by the field of the sluggard, by the vineyard of a man lacking sense, and behold, it was all overgrown with thorns, the ground was covered with nettles, and its stone wall had been broken down. Then I saw and considered it; I looked and received instruction. A little sleep, a little slumber, a little folding of the hands to rest, and poverty will come upon you like a robber, and want like an armed man." (Proverbs 24:30-34).

Is it wrong to ask you, how hard are you working for the Kingdom of Christ? How much of what you produce is really at the disposal of Christ to use for His Kingdom? When was the last time you turned the TV off to go outside and make contacts in your neighborhood? How hard do you work at being a friend to unbelievers?

To give you a clear but challenging picture of the largely dismal state of American Evangelicalism, let me quote Roy Moran:

"You would be hard pressed to find a state in the United States that has shown an increase in church attendance in the last decade. Even states such as California, Texas and Georgia—in which megachurches serve as models for many new church starts—couldn't report positive figures for church attendance in the last decade.... Of the estimated 400,000 US churches, only 3.5% are effective at expanding Jesus' kingdom, meaning fewer than 4 churches out of 100...."[26]

Does that sound like our churches are growing grapes or wild grapes to you? Since the Jesus of the New Testament is the God of the Old Testament, will you be one of the many who will be surprised when standing before Jesus and find that He

---

[26] Roy Moran, *Spent Matches*, 15

is "looking for fruit," just like He did when surveying the lives of His people Israel?

Why it Really Matters
Questions for Reflection (R) and ACTION (A)

1. While you may have quoted OT promises as your own, have you honestly considered that their often departures from the Faith could also be happening in your life & church? Discuss. (R)

2. Were you surprised by the statistics showing an Evangelical decline in the past decade? (R)

3. Do you have an effective way to witness to others? [27] (R)

4. Pick a 1-hour period of time you regularly spend alone at home and go somewhere you will have a chance to interact with strangers. Interact with 3 and journal the results (A)

---

[27] If you do not—please read Appendix 2

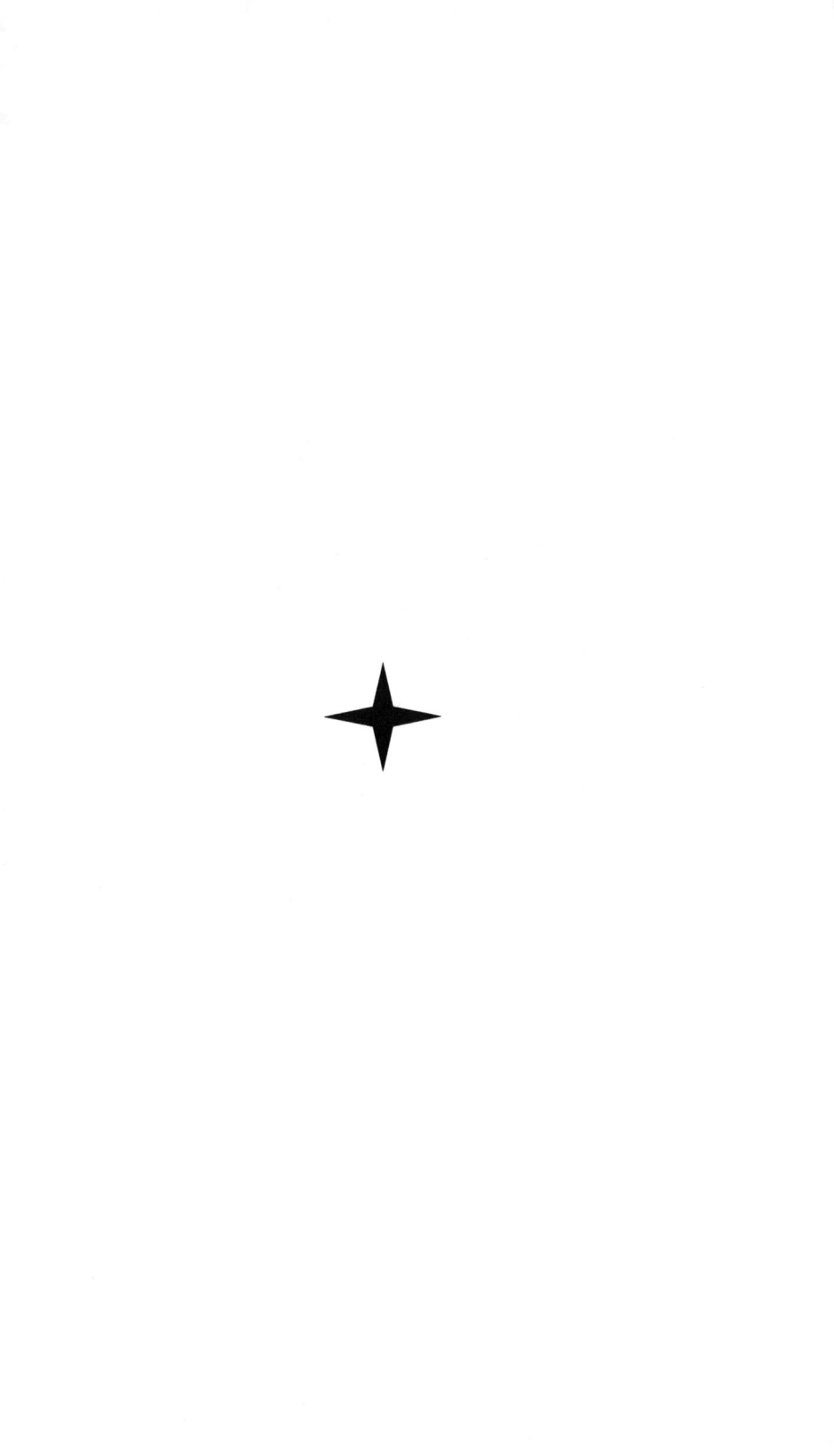

"Sowing in the morning, sowing seeds of kindness,
Sowing in the noontide and the dewy eve;
Waiting for the harvest, and the time of reaping,
We shall come rejoicing, bringing in the sheaves.

>   (Chorus)
>   "Bringing in the sheaves, bringing in the sheaves,
>   We shall come rejoicing, bringing in the sheaves;
>   Bringing in the sheaves, bringing in the sheaves,
>   We shall come rejoicing, bringing in the sheaves.

"Sowing in the sunshine, sowing in the shadows,
Fearing neither clouds nor winter's chilling breeze;
By and by the harvest, and the labor ended,
We shall come rejoicing, bringing in the sheaves.

"Going forth with weeping, sowing for the Master,
Though the loss sustained our spirit often grieves;
When our weeping's over, He will bid us welcome,
We shall come rejoicing, bringing in the sheaves."

A hymn by Knowles Shaw - 1874

Chapter 8
Sowing and Reaping in the Old Testament

A thorough study of fruitfulness and harvesting in both Old and New Testaments will help you better understand the strong conclusions I have drawn about unfruitful Christians today.

Did you know that there are over 500 texts in the Scriptures that allude to aspects of planting and harvesting? Bible writers of all ages are constantly alluding to agricultural phenomena and showing how they relate to the spiritual condition of both Old Testament and New Testament believers. In fact, it is hard to get a true picture of what God is saying to us without some understanding of the science of farming.

In this chapter, I will quote more Old Testament texts and briefly comment on them as they have direct bearing on the focus of this book. We must always see Christ through the blessings and promises and warnings of the Old Testament because Luke said, "And beginning with Moses and the Prophets, he interpreted to them in all the Scriptures the things concerning himself" (Luke 24:27). Old Testament texts must not be applied mainly or only as ways to motivate us to work harder. They always, when fully understood, point us to the perfect Messiah whose works were sinless and in whose righteousness, we are declared to be righteous.

God's harvest time is not always ours

> "When you come into the land and plant any kind of tree for food, then you shall regard its fruit as forbidden. Three years it shall be forbidden to you; it must not be eaten. And in the fourth year all its fruit shall be holy. An offering

of praise to the Lord. But in the fifth year you may eat of its fruit, to increase its yield for you: I am the Lord your God" (Leviticus 19:23-25).

You cannot understand the Bible and the children of Israel unless you take such laws seriously. The Mishnah[28] (the approved compilation of centuries of the oral law of Israel's elders written ca 200AD by Rabbi Judah the Patriarch) is a massive work composed of 6 major sections with many sub-sections in each section. Over 150 rabbinical teachers are quoted or referred to in the Mishnah. The whole work, when translated into English, composes nearly 800 pages. The first section is entitled, Zeraim or **Seeds**. Please get this, *seeds* come first. Before the other five sections dealing with the feasts, relationships, justice, holy things and sanctification, the Jewish mind focused on sowing and reaping in all of their complexities.

Now meditate on the Leviticus passage. And note from it these thoughts –

-Some fruit is forbidden, no matter how ripe it outwardly may appear to be

-God creates the fruit of the ground and expects His people to acknowledge and worship Him throughout its development and use. Praise precedes consumption, thereby demanding extreme self-control.

-Good fruit takes time to develop

-Obeying the law of God is more basic than satisfying our hunger

---

[28] The word Mishnah is derived from the Hebrew word "shanah" which means "repeat" and, so, refers to learning something by repetition. Mishnah is used of both teaching and the subject of the teaching which was communicated orally from teacher to disciple. Mastery came through correct repetition and application in groups.

-Jesus is tree and vine - our ever-producing, always ready-to-harvest LIFE. We need never wait for Him. He is always ready to bless and nourish us.

The fruit is not all for us

"For six years you shall sow your land and gather in its yield, but the seventh year you shall let it rest and lie fallow, that the poor of your people may eat; and what they leave the beasts of the field may eat. You shall do likewise with your vineyard, and with your olive orchard" (Exodus 23:10-11).

We may conclude from this passage:

-The ground needs a rest period, rather than constant and unending production

-What God gives us is also for others, too, especially those in need

-We must not forget our duty to feed God's creation, even when we see no personal gain from it

-Jesus is our Jubilee and, in Him, the best is yet to come!

Here is another and earlier text: "Joseph is a fruitful bough, a fruitful bough by a spring; his branches run over the wall" (Genesis 49:22). The entire blessing of Jacob upon Joseph (49:22-26) is incredibly suggestive. But I quote only the beginning, which portrays him as a fruitful, well-watered bough or cluster of grapes. Notice how the fruit multiplies and extends beyond its own property—over the wall. Joseph blessed many in and outside of the people of God. Many have seen in Joseph a type of Jesus the Messiah.

The one truly blessed by God

"Blessed is the man who walks not in the counsel of the wicked...but his delight is in the law of the Lord, and on his law he meditates day and night. *He is like a tree planted by streams of water that yields its fruit in its season, and its leaf does not wither. In all that he does, he prospers. The wicked are not so, but are like chaff which the wind drives away.* Therefore, the wicked will not stand in the judgment, nor sinners in the congregation of the righteous; for the Lord knows the way of the righteous, but the way of the wicked will perish" (Psalm 1)

The Psalms were collected and divided, eventually, into five sections[29] over centuries. The first and second psalms are viewed as the chosen introduction to the entire Book of Psalms as carrying in them the blessing of God (Ps 1:1and 2:12). The first psalm begins and the second psalm ends with the blessing—portraying these two psalms as framed by the word "blessed." One scholar notes, "... as the port of entry to the Psalter they (Pss 1&2) make clear that those who would find their own voice in the psalms and so would appropriate them as testimonies to their own faith must fit the profile of those called 'Blessed' here."[30] Now consider Psalm One.

-There are two types of people, the righteous and wicked

-The righteous learn, meditate on and cherish God's law

- As such, the righteous flourish like a well-watered tree

-The wicked, heeding the counsel of sinners, is like chaff. This is the husk around the fruitful kernel or grain, which must be removed

---

[29] Book 1 - 1-41; Book 2 - 42-72; Book 3 - 73-89; Book 4- 90-106, Book 5- 107-150
[30] John Stek in The NIV Bible Commentary, p. 788

-The righteous can stand before God but not the wicked. As they were weak and compromising on earth, so they shall not stand before God, but be driven away

-Jesus the Messiah or Anointed One (Psalm 2), is the truly blessed Man who lived upon His Father's Word and cherished His every command. No one is truly blessed apart from faith in Him. His righteousness or obedience is imputed to all who believe, because "no one is righteous, not even one," apart from Him

The Coming Messiah will be most fruitful!

Hundreds of years later, Jeremiah virtually repeats the blessing of Psalm 1 in a prophecy which states:

"Thus says the Lord: 'Cursed is the man who trusts in man and makes flesh his strength, whose heart turns away from the Lord. He is like a shrub in the desert, and shall not see any good come. He shall dwell in the parched places of the wilderness, in an uninhabited salt land. Blessed is the man who trusts in the Lord, whose trust is the Lord. He is like a tree planted by water, that sends out its roots by the stream, and does not fear when heat comes, for its leaves remain green, and is not anxious in the year of drought, for it does not cease to bear fruit'" (Jeremiah 23:5-8).

-You do not see many shrubs in the desert reproducing

-Note the themes of desert, parched places of wilderness, uninhabitable land being linked with one who trusts in man and is cursed by God

-Likewise, the themes tree by water, roots near stream, not fearing heat, green-leafed, not concerned with drought, constantly bearing fruit connected with those blessed ones who doubly trust in God

It did not take Jeremiah long before he also recognized that only the Messiah is truly righteous and eminently fruitful. So, in a section comparing true and false shepherds, he also wrote of the coming, fruitful Christ and the fruitfulness of all those who follow Him,

> "Woe to the shepherds who destroy and scatter the sheep of my pasture, declares the Lord.... I will gather the remnant of my flock out of all the countries where I have driven them, and I will bring them back to their fold, and they shall be fruitful and multiply. I will set shepherds over them who will care for them.... Behold, the days are coming declares the Lord, when I will raise up for David a righteous Branch, and he shall reign as king and deal wisely, and shall execute justice and righteousness in the land. In his days Judah will be saved and Israel will dwell securely. And this is the name by which he will be called, 'The Lord is our righteousness'" (Jeremiah 23:1-6).

The wisdom of sages addressed the importance of fruitfulness

Notice also some other pithy proverbs that spoke of the work of sowing and reaping:

> "He who gathers in summer is a prudent son, but he who sleeps in harvest is a son who brings shame (Proverbs 10:5)

> "I passed by the field of a sluggard, by the vineyard of a man lacking sense, and behold, it was all overgrown with thorns; the ground was covered with nettles, and its stone wall was broken down. Then I saw and considered it; a little sleep, a little slumber, a little folding of the hands to rest, and poverty will come upon you like a robber, and want like an armed man" (Proverbs 24:30-34)

Needless to say, the Old Testament Scriptures do not deal kindly with the unfruitful. The way of sin and foolishness is painted by the lives of the lazy, comfortable and unproductive in Israel. But, the OT Scriptures reveal a longing for the Messiah to come and heal the world of its death and unfruitfulness. Isn't part of His salvation, saving us from unfruitfulness?

When Jesus the Messiah came, what happened? He chose and trained Twelve Apostles, eleven of whom would change the course of the world by how bravely and lovingly they would devote themselves to a worldwide harvest. But we need not stop with the first century. Today, the fruitfulness of young disciples is truly incredible. To give you a glimpse of what can be, listen to missionary/author Jerry Trousdale:

> "God is creating a remarkable and unprecedented momentum of ministry in some of the least expected places in the Islamic world.... In our own ministry context, "unprecedented" is used to describe the following:
>
> -Multiple cases of entire mosques coming to faith;
>
> -Thousands of ordinary men and women being used by God to achieve seemingly impossible outcomes;
>
> -Tens of thousands of Muslim background Christians becoming dedicated intercessors who fast and pray for the gospel to penetrate the next community;
>
> -Muslim people groups that never had even one church among them now have more than fifty churches planted, and in some cases more than 100 churches—within two years of engagement;

-Former sheikhs, imams, and militant Islamists making up 20% or more of the new Christian leaders in Muslim regions."[31]

Jerry is a good friend and I have been incredibly blessed by being trained by him and some of these Muslim background disciples of Jesus. But, I look around me in the USA and I see well-educated and well-read Christians today are often unproductive, unfruitful, lazy and selfish with their use of time, money, vision and resources. But all while saying they believe in and follow Jesus! Jesus told us, "By their fruits you shall know them." Now let's move on to the New Testament and see if there is a continuity of the fruitfulness expected in the Old Testament. Or has the dawning of the great age of grace curbed God's demand and expectation for believers to bear fruit?

Why it Really Matters
Questions for Reflection (R) and ACTION (A)

1. How foundational to an accurate understanding of the Old Testament is a thorough understanding of the concepts of sowing and reaping? How foreign is that to you? (R)

2. Do you know many Christians who mirror the life and blessing of Psalm One? (R)

3. Since the Messiah was predicted to be fruitful, discuss how fruitful His followers are bound to be. (R)

4. Meet with your Christian accountability partner and share with him/her several concrete sins you have repented of since reading this book. (A)

5. State what repentance now looks like in your life, asking your accountability partner to hold you responsible to continue down those paths. (A)

---

[31] Jerry Trousdale in *Miraculous Movements*, 24-25

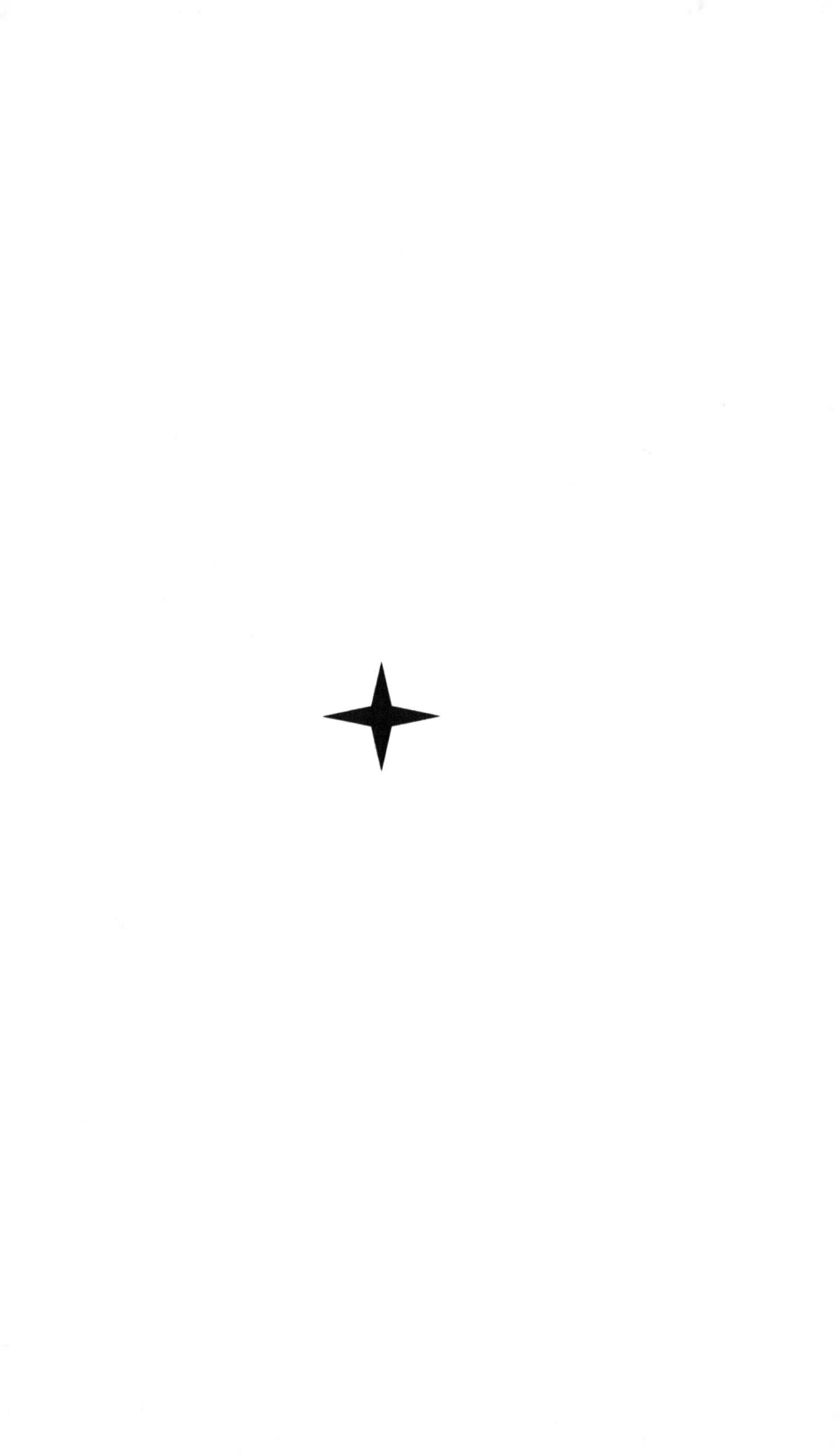

"O Lord, When Thou comest to look for fruit from the men of this Brotherhood, let not one of them disappoint Thee. Thou dost not like uselessness. We remember to have read that in Thy lifetime here upon earth, Thou didst cut one tree down because it bore no fruit. May we abound in fruit, plentiful and good, not merely ornamental. Thou hast planted us in a goodly place. May there be something in our lives to please Thee for all that Thou hast done for us. Amen."

Prayers of John Wanamaker (1838-1922)

Chapter 9
Cut it Down!

I want to follow the Old Testament lessons just covered with one specific message of Jesus from the Gospel of Luke. We all agree that God is unchangeable. His will does not vacillate. So, we might expect that what He expected of Israel, He desires of the Church, too.

Repent or else!

> "And he told this parable, 'A man had a fig tree planted in his vineyard, and he came seeking fruit on it and found none. And he said to the vinedresser, Look, for three years now I have come seeking fruit on this fig tree, and I find none. Cut it down. Why should it use up the ground?' And he answered him, 'Sir, let it alone this year also, until I dig around it and put on manure. Then if it should bear fruit next year, well and good; but if not, you can cut it down'" (Luke 13:6-9).

This parable is not found in any other Gospel. The NIV Study Bible offers this comment, "fig tree. Probably refers to the Jewish nation…, but it may also refer to an individual."[32] John MacArthur is a bit stronger, "fig tree. Often used as a symbol for Israel …. In this case, however, the parable's lesson about fruitlessness applies equally to the whole nation, and to each individual soul."[33]

I agree. Note how Luke has this parable following the passage where Jesus twice assures all individuals, "unless you repent, you will all likewise perish" (Luke 13:1-5). God demands

---
[32] NIV Study Bible, 1598
[33] MacArthur Study Bible, 1503

repentance from us all. And He expects that repentance to be visibly manifested by the bearing of true fruit.

Now, this being a parable, I do not want to press on every part of it too much. But I do not think it either wise or safe to do nothing with it. The danger, in our day, is to make it only yet another wonderful picture of the grace of Christ our Lord. When this passage is preached on or studied, certainly it is right to see, in Christ, the vinedresser who pleaded for grace. The one who asked for one more year. But, please do not err in seeing Jesus as here forgiving fruitlessness, for that is not what the parable teaches. Matthew Henry captured this long ago,

> "Christ is the great Intercessor; he ever lives, interceding.... Now, observe what it is he prays for, and that is a reprieve: 'Lord, let it alone this year also.' He doth not pray, 'Lord, let it never be cut down,' but, 'Lord not now....' We owe it to Christ, the Great Intercessor, that barren trees are not cut down immediately.... Reprieves of mercy are but for a time; 'Let it alone this year also,' a short time, but a sufficient time to make trial. When God has borne long, we may hope he will bear yet little longer, but we cannot expect he should bear always.... Observe here, that though God bears long, he will not bear always with unfruitful professors; his patience will have an end, and, if it be abused, will give way to that wrath which will have no end. Barren trees will certainly be cut down at last and cast into the fire."[34]

What kind of fruitfulness?

I would like to have us look at this very serious passage keeping in mind all the other chapters in this book which have preceded it. So let me ask a couple leading questions:

---

[34] Matthew Henry's Commentary on the Whole Bible, 1870-1871

1. What was the owner looking for from the fig tree? He was looking for fruit. That is for figs. Not one fig but for several, at least. Fig trees are expected to produce figs. And, of course, when the pit of one of these figs would be planted into the soil, it is with the hope that an entire fig-bearing tree would be produced. One fig holds in it the seed to reproduce an entire fig-laden tree.

2. What is the meaning of "fruitfulness" in this story? The owner implies for us what fruitfulness is. Fruitfulness is reproducing fruit. You see, the tree may have been otherwise quite beautiful. Even full of leaves giving shade for those who would sit under it in the heat of the day. It might have been a haven for birds, offering a wonder of sights as mother takes care of the baby birds and all make beautiful noise for the onlookers. I could go on, but I think you get my point. The owner wanted fruit that could be eaten or sold or planted. That was the primary meaning of "fruitfulness" to him. He did not plant the tree for its other secondary benefits.

Since this parable is selected by Luke to follow Christ's severe warnings about personal repentance, should we not take it quite personally? So please respond to this unavoidable and fateful question: Are you willing to repent of an unfruitful life? (Your repentance might be helped by reading Appendix 4 – Faith without WHICH works is dead?). Of course, your life has had some good features; but, has it failed to reproduce? How can true repentance in you look like anything else than sharing your faith and making disciples of Christ?

Please understand that my perpetual call for repentance does not flow from an anti-grace spirit. It takes grace to repent! And life change can be both quick and thorough because of the reality of the gospel. We are proclaimed righteous by faith in Jesus. We are forgiven only through believing and trusting in His atoning death. The gospel, rightly understood, then propels us forward into a life of devoted works of love. When our sins are dealt with daily by "preaching the gospel to ourselves," we embrace repentance and, then, may be filled with the fruitful Spirit of God! Only a gospel-embracing people can follow Jesus as His disciples. The gospel allows us to be honest about our sins, our needs, our vast inadequacies. Because it rescues us from all of those in Christ by the resurrection power of the Spirit. This demanding message is not an advancement of works over grace. In fact, it is just the opposite!

We have seen how, when looking at Israel, "God looked for fruit." Do you not think that God is also looking for you to love and share the gospel with others who are perishing in their sins? God is watching you. And He will have the final word. I pray that it will not be, "Cut it down!"

Why it Really Matters
Questions for Reflection (R) and ACTION (A)

1. Have you ever prayed a request like the prayer of John Wanamaker? If not, why not? (R)

2. Discuss what you think is the relevance to you between cutting the tree down and letting it live for one more year. (R)

3. Think about and discuss the following Gospel Hymn (R)

"Lord, lay some soul upon my heart,
And love that soul through me;
And may I bravely do my part
To win that soul to Thee.

Some soul for Thee. Some soul for Thee
This is my earnest plea;

Help me each day, on life's highway
To win some soul for Thee.

Lord, lead me to some soul in sin,
And grant that I may be
Endued with power and love to win
That soul, dear Lord, for Thee.

To win that soul for Thee, my Lord,
Will be my constant prayer;
That when I've won Thy full reward
I'll with that dear one share."

A hymn by BB McKinney (1886-1952)

4. Begin to journal every contact you have with an unbeliever daily that leads to some witness of Christ (A)

5. Pray for those people and consider what you are doing as planting seed and watering it (A)

"Far and near the fields are teeming

With the waves of ripened grain;
Far and near their gold is gleaming
O'er the sunny slope and plain.

(Chorus)

"Lord of harvest, send forth reapers!
Hear us, Lord; to Thee we cry.
Send them now the sheaves to gather,
Ere the harvest-time pass by.

"Send them forth with morn's first beaming;
Send them in the noontide's glare;
When the sun's last rays are gleaming,
Thou shalt come with joy untold.

"O thou whom thy Lord is sending,
Gather now the sheaves of gold;
Heav'nward then at evening wending,
Thou shalt come with joy untold."

A hymn by James O Thompson (1834-1917)

Chapter 10

Sowing and Reaping in the Gospels

The New Testament was written almost exclusively by Jewish believers.[35] As such, most of them would have had an intimate understanding of the Old Testament Scriptures. So, it is of no surprise to see that their writings also are filled with allusions to farming. Even though we have had a hint in previous chapters, the question of most interest to us is, "Did they also see fruitfulness as a characteristic of true faith?"

John the Baptizer – *Bear fruit or perish!*

We will start with John the Baptizer, the great herald of the coming Messiah. His ministry was so important that all four of the gospel writers write of him. Mark begins his Gospel focusing on John! From the relatively few words that we have from him, it is significant that the following is recorded in Matthew's Gospel:

> "But when he saw many of the Pharisees and Sadducees coming to his baptism, he said to them, 'You brood of vipers! Who warned you to flee from the wrath to come? Bear fruit in keeping with repentance.... Even now the axe is laid to the root of the trees. Every tree therefore that does not bear good fruit is cut down and thrown into the fire. I baptize you with water for repentance, but he who is coming after me is mightier than I, whose sandals I am not worthy to carry. He will baptize you with the Holy Spirit and fire. His winnowing fork is in his hand, and he will clear his threshing floor and gather his wheat into the

---

[35] Luke was the only non-Jewish writer, being, most likely, a Roman citizen according to most NT scholars

barn, but the chaff he will burn with unquenchable fire'" (Matthew 3:7-12).

Dear reader, what do YOU think that message meant? How much explanation from me does it require? Those are frightening, thunderous words! But of the thousands of words which John no doubt spoke, the great issue which John addressed to both the leaders and the crowds was that of true repentance. What depicts real repentance, to John? Good fruit. And what is good fruit? Of course, the fruit depicting repentance indicates a dramatic change of character. Like a life filled with radical expressions of generosity rather than greed and extortion (Luke 3:11-13). But does fruitfulness, in John's mind, stop there?

Not if we let the Bible itself answer the question! What actually happened when the Lord later fulfilled John's prophecy and baptized them with the Holy Spirit? What was the actual fruit? You know the story as it is revealed in Acts 2. When they were baptized with the Spirit, **they shared their faith** in praise verbally with others! In an unmistakable way. They spoke miraculously in the languages of the foreigners who were on pilgrimage to Jerusalem for the festival of Pentecost. Then Peter, who was also baptized with the Spirit, addressed the gathering crowd, saying, "Repent and be baptized every one of you for the forgiveness of sins and you will receive the gift of the Holy Spirit" (Acts 2:38). What fruit flowed from Peter's preaching? Luke records, "And there were added that day about 3,000 souls" (Acts 2:41).

In fact, when Luke first summarized what normal life in the Church of Jerusalem looked like (Acts 2:42-47), he concluded saying, "And the Lord added to their number day by day those who were being saved" (Acts 2:47). Thousands were being saved, becoming reproducing disciples of Jesus Christ. The numerical growth was so staggering that Luke introduced a new word. Instead of believers being merely "added, "Jesus began "multiplying" believers.[36] That is what happens when each disciple begins to make disciples. The Church multiplies! But, note, the Word says, "the Lord added" (Acts 2:47). The disciples were sharing, but the present, reigning, conquering Christ was the One who was adding to the Church! When disciples follow Jesus, He leads them to people of peace, prepared by the Spirit and ready to receive the Word.

Jesus on Fruitfulness – *This is the <u>true</u> test of character*

I will focus on just a couple of Jesus' statements concerning fruit bearing right now. Just read carefully these words of warning from your Lord and Savior, the God before whom you will stand:

> "Beware of false prophets, who come to you in sheep's clothing, but inwardly are ravenous wolves. You will recognize them by their fruits. Are grapes gathered from thorn bushes, or figs from thistles? So, every healthy tree bears good fruit, but the diseased tree bears bad fruit. Every tree that does not bear good fruit is cut down and thrown into the fire. Thus, you will recognize them by their fruits" (Matthew 7:15-20).

Evangelical False Prophets?

False prophets should be tested in at least two ways: (1) by whether their prophecies coincide with other words from God, and (2) by whether their predictions come to pass. You might not think you have ever encountered a false prophet. BUT, many evangelical ministers and their followers proclaim to new Christians dogmatic statements about their future after the person makes a profession of faith. They say things like:

---

[36] See Acts 6:1,7; 7:17; 9:31; 12:24

"You are saved!"

"You have eternal life and nothing can change that!"

"You are now bound for heaven, no matter what you do, because you are saved by grace!"

Let me ask you—**might not these be falsely prophesying who declare to those who have "prayed the prayer" that they are bound for the Promised Land? How can they be so sure? There is no fruit yet flowing from their lives except a few words.** And Jesus warned them (and us) about the uncertain nature of religious words when He immediately followed these statements, saying,

> "Not everyone who says to me, 'Lord, Lord,' will enter the kingdom of heaven, but the one who does the will of my Father who is in heaven. On that day many will say to me, 'Lord, Lord did we not prophesy in your name, and cast out demons in your name, and do many mighty works in your name?' And then I will declare to them, 'I never knew you; depart from me, you workers of lawlessness'" (Matthew 7:21-23).

So, those who place such a great emphasis on "getting them to pray the sinner's prayer," might, quite unknowingly, be at times the devil's tool. As are some who cast out demons and work other supernatural deeds. Peter prophesied falsely when he told Jesus, "Far be it from you, Lord! This (suffering and death) shall never happen to you!" (Matthew 16:22). Jesus shocked him and all the others by exclaiming to Peter, eyeball-to-eyeball, "Get behind me, Satan! You are a hindrance to me. For you are not setting your mind on the things of God, but on the things of man" (Matthew 16:23).

"An enemy has done this!"

Another message regarding sowing and reaping which Jesus gave follows:

"The kingdom of heaven may be compared to a man who sowed good seed in his field, but while he was sleeping his enemy came and sowed weeds among the wheat and went away. So when the plants grew up and bore grain, then the weeds appeared also. And the servants of the house came and said to him, 'Master, did you not sow good seed in your field? How then does it have weeds?' He said to them, 'An enemy has done this.' So the servants said to him, 'Do you want us to go and gather them?' But he said, 'No, lest in gathering the weeds you root up the wheat along with them. Let both grow together until the harvest, and at harvest time, I will tell the reapers, Gather the weeds first and bind them in bundles to be burned, but gather the wheat into my barn'" (Matthew 13:24-30)

Let's stick with what appears to be the obvious from this parable.

-Jesus has an enemy, who is determined to mix weeds into His field

-It is hard for reapers to tell the wheat from the weeds until they grow for a while

-The weeds which grew in His field (Church?) will be identified, bundled and burned

-The wheat will be gathered into His barn (heaven/kingdom)

Satan is not at work only in the world. He is at work in churches, too. He is a planter or a proponent of "church growth!" So, we must take care how our churches grow!

Our purpose in writing this book is not to deal exhaustively with the topic of fruitfulness in the Bible. It is, rather, to speak fairly to it, yet in a brief and personal way. I could continue beyond the Gospels into the writings of Paul and all of the other New Testament writers and show that they also focused on it.[37] I will conclude this chapter with one last statement from Jesus.

"Every branch that does not bear fruit"

> "I am the true vine and my Father is the vine dresser. Every branch in me that does not bear fruit, he takes away, and every branch that does bear fruit he prunes that it may bear more fruit.... I am the vine; you are the branches. Whoever abides in me and I in him, he it is that bears much fruit, for apart from me you can do nothing. If anyone does not abide in me, he is thrown away like a branch and withers; and the branches are gathered and thrown into the fire, and burned.... You did not choose me, but I chose you and appointed you that you should go and bear fruit and that your fruit should abide, so that whatever you ask the Father in my name, he may give it to you" (John 15:1-6,16)

These words were spoken by Jesus to the apostles on the eve before His crucifixion. They were seared into the memory of John and the others. Again, though a parabolic lesson, there must be important basic truths here for the apostles and for us. To me, the text is clear:

> -Fruitfulness/reproduction is the will of the Father and the Son for all who follow Christ

> -It is possible to be outwardly connected with Jesus (in me) without having the life of the Vine (Christ) animating and growing you. One may be a church member and yet be lost

> -All who do not bear fruit, without exception, are ultimately cut off and destroyed

---

[37] See such important texts as Rom. 1:13; 2 Cor 9:6, 10; Gal. 5:22-23, 6:7-8; Eph 5:11; Phil 1:22; Col 1:6, 10; Titus 3:14; Heb 12:11, 13:15; James 3:17, 5:18; 2 Pet 1:8; Jude 12; Rev. 22:2, 17

-The life of Christ flows into and through all who are vitally connected to Him

-To bear fruit in this passage means to make other disciples (John 15:16). "Fruit that remains" cannot mean here, our merely growing in Christ-like qualities or "the fruit of the Spirit" (Gal. 5:22-23). Because the fruit here "remains," unlike our "love, joy, peace, etc." which fluctuate all the time. Sometimes we are patient and other times we "lose it" and give way to anger. Disciples, however, that Christ makes through us "remain."

The barren bride of Christ?

Believers are referred to as "the bride of Christ" (2 Cor. 11:2: Rev. 21:2, 9). Do you really think that the bride of Christ can be barren or fruitless? I don't. The whole Bible is concluded by the revelation of Jesus to John saying, "The Spirit and the bride say, 'Come.'" (Rev 22:17). As one who would identify yourself as His bride, how often do you invite others to come? How fruitful has your union with Christ been?

Why it Really Matters
Questions for Reflection (R) and ACTION (A)

1. Do you think John the Baptist's warnings are relevant to Christians? (R)

2. Discuss whether it is possible to be a false prophet when you are just trying to give a young Christian the assurance of their salvation. (R)

3. Consider Mark 1:23 where we see "the devil in the synagogue," and discuss in what ways the devil (or demons) might affect our church services. (R)

4. In the light of this chapter, read and discuss John 4:36 (R)

5. Consider the words of the following gospel song: (R)

Rescue the perishing, care for the dying,
Snatch them in pity from sin and the grave;
Weep o'er the erring one, lift up the fallen,
Tell them of Jesus, the mighty to save.

> *(chorus)*
> *Rescue the perishing, care for the dying,*
> *Jesus is merciful, Jesus will save.*

Though they are slighting Him, still He is waiting,
Waiting the penitent child to receive;
Plead with them earnestly, plead with them gently;
He will forgive if they only believe.

Down in the human heart, crushed by the tempter,
Feelings lie buried that grace can restore;
Touched by a loving heart, wakened by kindness,
Chords that were broken will vibrate once more.

Rescue the perishing, duty demands it;
Strength for thy labor the Lord will provide;
Back to the narrow way patiently win them;
Tell the poor wand'rer a Savior has died.

A hymn by Fanny Crosby 1869

6. Interview 3 Christians (using your journal) to discover if they have any real interest in being a disciple of Jesus (A)

7. Pray for those who are and are not wanting to "follow Christ" in a life of radical obedience (A)

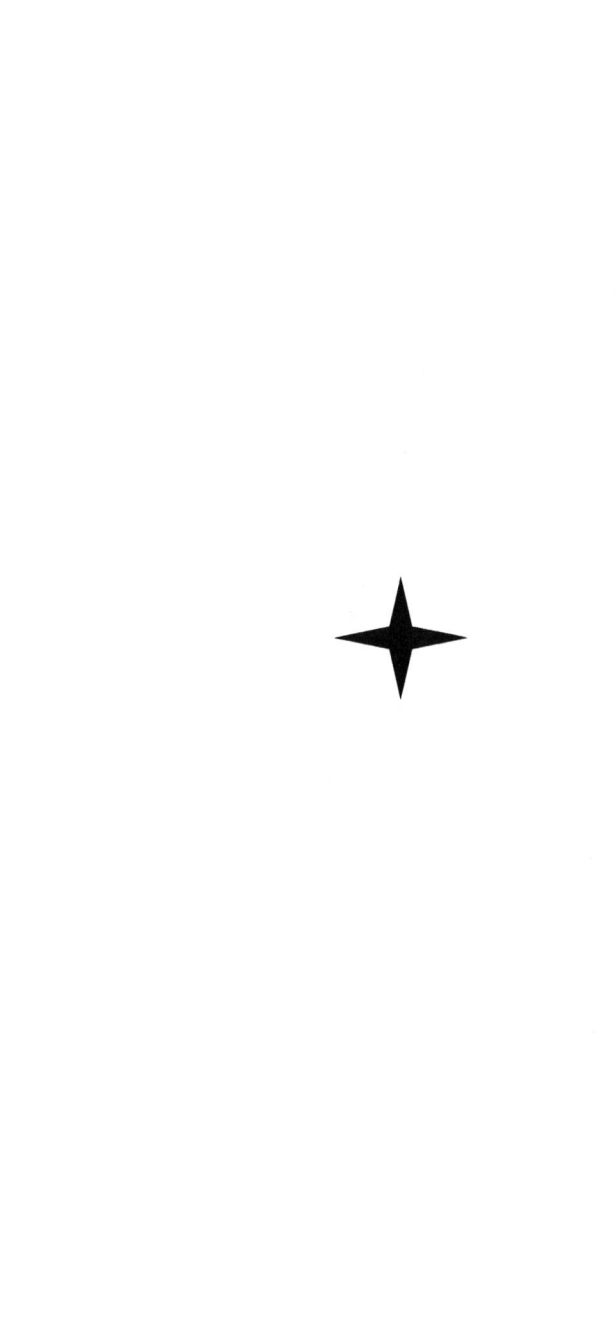

"O Zion, haste, thy mission high fulfilling,
To tell to all the world that God is light;
That He who made all nations is not willing
One soul should perish, lost in shades of night.

>   (chorus)
>   Publish glad tidings, tidings of peace;
>   Tidings of Jesus, redemption and release.

Behold how many thousands still are lying,
Bound in the darksome prison house of sin,
With none to tell them of the Savior's dying,
Or of the life He died for them to win.

Proclaim to every people, tongue, and nation
That God, in whom they live and move, is love;
Tell how He stooped to save His lost creation,
And died on earth that we might live above.

Give of thy sons to bear the message glorious;
Give of thy wealth to speed them on their way;
Pour out thy soul for them in prayer victorious;
And all thou spendest Jesus will repay."

Mary A Thompson 1868

Chapter 11
Good or Bad Soil?

Jesus often chose to speak to the great crowds in parables or by lessons utilizing familiar objects and events to them. The **Parable of the Seed and the Sower** is one of only a few of His 40 recorded parables to be included in all three of what are called "the Synoptic Gospels" (Matt. 13, Mark 4 & Luke 8).[38] John's Gospel contains no parables. Many have viewed this one as the most important of all of Jesus' parables, for several reasons. I will state only two. First, Jesus asked, "Do you not understand this parable? How then will you understand all the parables?" (Mark 4:13). And by that question, He seems to be suggesting that its basic truths underlie all of the others. To misinterpret this one could lead to misinterpreting them all. Secondly, this is the one parable concerning which Jesus gives a full and complete interpretation or meaning which was recorded by all three Gospel writers. All three writers believed it was an indispensable key for all of their readers to have the true interpretation of this one parable.

Do YOU understand the secret of God's kingdom?

It was through parables that Jesus taught His disciples "the secret of the kingdom of God" (Mark 4:11). Jesus told them that secret "has not been given to them" (the great crowds- Matt 13:11; Mk 4:11; Lk 8:9). So, many of those who heard Him did not grasp fully the importance of what He taught. But, the disciples were different. Jesus said, "blessed are your eyes, for they see, and your ears, for they hear" (Matt. 13:16).

---

[38] Matthew, Mark and Luke are called "Synoptic" because they are largely similar in how they view the life of Christ. The 4 other parables recorded in all Synoptics are: The lamp under a bowl, New cloth on old coat/new wine in old wineskins and The tenants.

So, here's a big question to you—*Do you get the meaning of this foundational teaching of Jesus concerning the nature of His Kingdom?* Do you perceive who is "in" and who is "out"? Who is close and who is far? And how it can appear that we are safe when, actually, we are still in great danger. If it was so important that the first disciples, who read it, understood this parable, it is vital for you also to "have eyes to see and ears to hear." So, please read this both carefully and prayerfully:

> "And he began to teach beside the sea. And a very large crowd gathered about him…and he was teaching them many things in parables, and in his teaching he said to them: Listen! Behold, a sower went out to sow. And as he sowed, some seed fell along the path, and the birds came and devoured it. Other seed fell on rocky ground, where it did not have much soil, and immediately it sprang up, since it had no depth of soil. And when the sun rose, it was scorched, and since it had no root, it withered away. Other seed fell among thorns, and the thorns grew up and choked it, and it yielded no grain. And other seeds fell into good soil and produced grain, growing up and increasing and yielding thirtyfold and sixtyfold and a hundredfold. And he said, He who has ears to hear, let him hear" (Mark 4:1-9)

Before we quote the meaning that Jesus gave to this vitally important parable, let me ask you—*Which of the four kinds of soil do you think depicts you?* Are you (1) along the path, (2) rocky soil, (3) thorn-infested soil, or (4) good soil? James later commanded his readers, "Therefore put away all filthiness and rampant wickedness, and receive with meekness the implanted word, which is able to save your souls" (James 1:21). Now, for the meaning of the parable as Jesus explained it:

> "The sower sows the word. And these are the ones along the path, where the word is sown: when they hear, Satan immediately comes and takes away the word that is sown in them. And these are the ones sown on rocky ground:

the ones who, when they hear the word, immediately receive it with joy. And they have no root in themselves, but endure for a while, then, when tribulation or persecution arises on account of the word, immediately they fall away. And others are the ones sown among thorns. They are those who hear the word, but the cares of the world and the deceitfulness of riches and the desires for other things enter in and choke the word, and it proves unfruitful. But those that were sown on the good soil are the ones who hear the word and accept it and bear fruit, thirtyfold and sixtyfold and a hundredfold" (Mark 4:14-20)

Do YOU really get it?

Do you have eyes to see the obvious? To me, applying this parable to ourselves today leads me to at least the ten following conclusions:

1. It is not enough to "go to church." What matters is what you do with the Word that you hear. What place has the "good news of the kingdom" found in your life?

2. Jesus mentioned 4 different ways to receive the Gospel—and only one of them is okay

3. The devil and his host are in the church and, trying to mess with how you hear the Word.

4. Some hear the Word and immediately forget it

5. Some hear the word with great emotion and joy—but with no permanent or lasting fruitfulness. They give up following Jesus when seriously opposed for it. Has your faith been so secretive that you have never been persecuted for it? Then how do you know you really have been saved?

6. Has the world or Jesus won over your heart? What do you desire more—the things of this life or obeying Jesus?

7. Does money matter more than Jesus to you? Jesus declared, "You cannot serve God and money" (Matt. 6:24)

8. To bear fruit for only a while is not enough. To have a testimony about "yesteryear" and no ongoing fruitfulness is a very dangerous thing.

9. Only ONE type of soil leads to the Kingdom of God, to true salvation.

10. Only those who reproduce are "good soil," and Jesus looks for a great harvest of 30, 60 and 100 times!

Many Christians today have embraced a culture that includes Jesus, while rejecting a life and lifestyle devoted to serving Him. And they are assured that they are saved. They have eternal life. They are part of the Kingdom of God. It does not matter if they have effectively witnessed and reproduced at all. They have been declared, "justified" and been given assurance of their salvation. They would claim to be Christians; but, hesitate to claim that they are the disciples of Jesus. (See Appendix 5 – Christians should **fear** standing before God unfruitfully)

True disciples take up their cross and multiply. If you desire to multiply, you need to be discipled. To be trained. To become accountable to another who is following Jesus and will demonstrate to you what that demands and looks like in your culture. There are probably some around you willing to help, too. Look for them first within your church. Then elsewhere if you can find no one. We are willing to help you as best we can.[39]

---

[39] Contact us if you desire to be disciple and can find no one to help: ed.gross@comcast.net;

Why it Really Matters
Questions for Reflection (R) and ACTION (A)

1. Before reading this chapter, discuss how you interpreted the Parable of the Sower and the Seed. (R)

2. If 30, 60 and 100-fold means something other than making other disciples – what does it mean? (R)

3. How many of the Christians that you know are regularly proclaiming the gospel and making disciples as a result of it? (R)

4. What are you going to DO about your own level of soul-winning fruitfulness? (R)

5. Now go and do it, journaling the results (A)

"The viability of the Christian faith, it turns out, is intimately related to engagement in discipleship. Jesus did not spend three years modeling the discipleship process because He wasn't sure how else to end His time on earth. The writers of Scripture did not capture Jesus' words on the meaning of discipleship and the related efforts of the apostles for lack of creative ideas.... The strength and influence of the church is wholly dependent upon its commitment to true discipleship. Producing transformed lives, and seeing those lives reproduced in others, is a core challenge to believers and to the local church."

George Barna (Growing True Disciples) 2001

Chapter 12
Your kingdom come....

When Jesus sat down and distinguished His life and teaching from the way of all other rabbis, He spoke about many subjects.[40] One of them was prayer. He taught the disciples to say, "Your kingdom come. Your will be done, on earth as it is in heaven" (Matt 6:10).

Understanding "The Lord's Prayer"

Christians have uttered these words in worship for centuries. You have probably memorized this prayer. But have you really asked yourself these questions about this most important of all prayers...

> *Do I understand the meaning and importance of the kingdom of God?*
>
> *Is the universal kingdom of God more important to me than my reputation, my schedule, my assets, my little "kingdom"?*
>
> *Does my life show devotion to bringing God's kingdom (or rule) over people and places where it does not exist?*

Unless you wrongly think sheer repetition matters greatly to God[41], you probably should make sure that you understand the meaning of the words you use when you are praying. Your mind and heart must embrace and desire the very words you are uttering to God when you pray.

---

[40] For a fuller handling of Christ's Sermon on the Mount in light of New Testament Discipleship see *Are You a Christian or a Disciple* chapter 13 and Its Appendix 3 - "50 Commands of Jesus for Disciples Today to Memorize"

[41] Jesus commanded, "And when you pray, do not heap up empty phrases as the Gentiles do, for they think that they will be heard for their many words." (Matt 6:7)

The whole premise of this book, when embraced, gives a clarity and power to The Lord's Prayer that rarely otherwise happens. The advancement of Christ's kingdom should be a matter of great importance to all of His followers. Dallas Willard clearly and concisely defines God's kingdom as follows:

> "God's own 'kingdom' or 'rule' is the range of his effective will, where what he wants done is done." [42]

How can we pray diligently for that to which we do not devote ourselves? How can we rightly pray for His kingdom to come to others if we have not yielded our life to it? If we are not committed to sharing "the good news of the kingdom" with others?

In this prayer we ask for our "daily bread" to be provided by the Father. So, it has become the practice of Christians down through the ages to pray this prayer every day. Prayer for **daily** bread implies a **daily** asking. We almost shudder to think of a day passing without eating. But how many days has it been since you have shared Jesus, the "bread of life" with another hungry soul?

Some hard questions

Following the petition about the extension of God's kingdom, comes "Your will be done, on earth as it is in heaven." Here are some questions about this request…

-Have I understood this request in connection with what precedes it?

-Do I understand that God's kingdom cannot come where His will is not done?

- Do I seek to pray for and perform God's will mainly as it advances His kingdom?

---

[42] Dallas Willard in *The Divine Conspiracy*, 25

-Do I know and truly desire what God's will is for me, my neighbor and the earth?

-Have I ever considered how angels perform God's bidding, His will, when they are sent out on a mission?

-Does my life reflect even remotely the fulfillment of God's will on earth that a mission of an angel reveals when sent on a mission by God to earth?

We know that the Bible declares, "God is not wishing that any should perish but that all should come to repentance" (2 Peter 3:9). Does that not reveal His will? We know that God commanded the prophet, "Say to them, as I live, declares the Lord God, I have no pleasure in the death of the wicked, but that the wicked turn from his way and live; turn back, turn back from your evil ways, for why will you die O house of Israel?" (Ezekiel 33:11).

The Lord's Prayer is to be prayed for "us" and "our," not for "me" and "my." It begins with God's concerns and places ours second. How different is this prayer from the prayers which so many Christians pray today! And here is another prayer that is very different from what we might hear at our prayer meetings. It was prayed by the famous Philadelphia merchant one Sunday when he commenced the Sunday School classes for that day.

> "O God of all blessings, do Thou pity and visit us today, as we wait in the courts of Thine house, otherwise we shall faint and fall and be dead....
>
> "O that we had hearkened unto Thee long ago, for then, by this time, we might have been stalwart men, made giant-like and mighty by the indwelling of Thy Spirit, instead of the poor, shallow, cunning, shuffling men that we are. Disarm the devil and sweep him off the earth. Awaken the slumbering Church; then condescend to manage it Thyself, that Thy plans be not hampered and Thy glory be not dimmed, among the children of men. Amen."

Dear reader, how can we utter the Lord's Prayer and read Wanamaker's and not make disciples of those willing, ready and able to be discipled around us? Angels live for nothing more than to perform His will. They have not been redeemed, like we have. For us to be fruitless, to not make disciples is unthinkable! Yet how many Christians pray this prayer, even daily, with no intention, no desire, no fire of love and gratitude burning within them to actually do it themselves? God have mercy!

Why it Really Matters
Questions for Reflection and ACTION

1. Discuss the quote from Christian demographer, George Barna. (R)

2. Do you pray the Lord's Prayer daily? Why or why not? (R)

3. Does your heart resonate with the prayer of Wanamaker? (R)

4. Read Matthew 21:28-31 and ask yourself, "Which son am I?" (R)

5. Some are offended by the following hymn. Are you? (R)

Far, far away, in heathen darkness dwelling,
Millions of souls forever may be lost;
Who, who will go, salvation's storytelling,
Looking to Jesus, counting not the cost?

(Chorus)

All pow'r is given unto me,
All pow'r is given unto me,
"Go ye into all the world and preach the gospel,
And lo, I am with you always."

See o'er the world, wide open doors inviting:
Soldiers of Christ, arise and enter in!
Christians, awake! your forces all uniting,
Send forth the Gospel, break the chains of sin.

"Why will ye die?" the voice of God is calling,
"Why will ye die?" re-echo in His name:
Jesus hath died to save from death appalling,
Life and salvation therefore go proclaim.

A hymn by James McGranahan (1840-1907)

6. To help God's kingdom come and His will be done, Christians must become disciples who make disciples. If you want a 3 month "Christian-to-Disciple" outline to start with a group of friends, go to: www.disciplesgo.com and download it for free (A)

"The Great Commission is not a special calling or a gift of the Spirit, it is a command—an obligation incumbent upon the whole community of faith. There are no exceptions. Bank presidents and automobile mechanics, physicians and school teachers, theologians and homemakers—everyone who believes on Christ has a part in His work."

Robert Coleman (The Master Plan of Discipleship) 1987

Chapter 13

Christ's Final Command

The first chapter of this book focused on God's first command. This last chapter on the last command which the incarnate Son of God gave to His disciples.[43] That final command is better known as The Great Commission. We want to conclude our little book by giving three final and powerful arguments proving the absolute importance of all true Christians or disciples of Jesus to devote themselves daily to sharing their faith and producing "fruit that remains." The first argument is simply this: all of the Gospel writers conclude their stories of Christ's life by repeating His command that His followers should go into the world as His witnesses, proclaiming the good news and making disciples of those who believe. Is this not enormously significant?

As written by Matthew

The Great Commission is stated in all four Gospels in the following words:

> "Then Jesus came to them and said, 'All authority in heaven and on earth has been given to me. Therefore, go and make disciples of all nations, baptizing them in the name of the Father and of the Son and of the Holy Spirit, and teaching them to obey everything I have commanded

---

[43] Following the Great Commission, Jesus commanded His disciples to "stay in the city until you are clothed with power from on high" (Lk 24:49). That was a command which was fulfilled on the Day of Pentecost (Acts 2) when they were "all filled with the Holy Spirit" (Acts 2:4). So, technically, the final command was related to waiting for the power of the Spirit, as He is essential for the fulfillment of the Great Commission. (Acts 1:8)

you. And surely I am with you always, to the very end of the age'" (Matthew 28:19-20),

These are the final or last words of Jesus in the Gospel of Matthew. We are left with this command. The command is "make disciples." The way to do so is by going, baptizing and teaching obedience in His very real and powerful presence. His powerful presence is promised to all disciple-makers until this age ends.

As written by Mark

"He said to them, 'Go into all the world and proclaim the gospel to the whole creation. Whoever believes and is baptized will be saved, but whoever does not believe will be condemned" (Mark 16:15-16)

This is Christ's last command in the last chapter of Mark's Gospel. They are to go and proclaim the gospel. We are grateful that the ESV translation uses "proclaim" rather than "preach," because in many cultures only preachers preach. And relatively few Christians are preachers. Whereas, all creation is impacted by the Gospel, the proper response by humans is to "believe." This is more than mental knowledge. It leads naturally to the outward obedience of baptism. Baptism was the moment of public confession that the one baptized belonged, was totally committed to the name into which he/her was baptized. Jesus commanded baptism to mark and unite believers. But, note carefully, it is not essential for salvation, because "whoever does not believe will be condemned." True faith saves! Finally note, Jesus promises that God will "condemn" those who do not believe. That thought alone should propel us to share the gospel with others!

As written by Luke

> "These are my words that I spoke to you while I was still with you, that everything written about me in the Law of Moses and the Prophets and the Psalms must be fulfilled. Then he opened their minds to understand the Scriptures and said to them, Thus it is written that the Christ should suffer and on the third day rise from the dead, and that repentance and forgiveness of sins should be proclaimed in his name to all nations, beginning from Jerusalem. You are **witnesses** of these things. (Luke 24:44-47)

The life and work of Jesus fulfilled ancient prophecies. They can only be rightly understood when connected with His coming and the redemption which He would bring to the earth. The Apostles were to be witnesses of Jesus' great work of redemption. We get the word "martyr" from the Greek word for "witnesses" (*martures*). Christ said His witnesses would focus on the two great needs throughout the earth: repentance and forgiveness. All humans need to repent of their sins so that they might be forgiven. Without repentance, then, there is no forgiveness. Are you a witness leading other to repentance and its eternal fruit—forgiveness? We cannot speak of repentance if we cannot speak of sin! The moment sin is mentioned, there are cries of "don't judge me!" "I'm not that bad." The trump word today is "tolerance." And to share the gospel with another is often viewed as an intolerant, power move. So, many Christians shun witnessing as Christ commanded, because our culture does not accommodate the exclusiveness of true Christianity.

As written by John

> "Jesus said to them again, Peace be with you. As the Father has sent me, even so I am sending you. And when he had said this, he breathed on them and said, Receive the Holy Spirit." (John 20:21-22)

Jesus came in peace (shalom) and sends out His disciples in peace. They are to go even as Jesus went. They have been with Him and seen how He went in the power of the Spirit. Now they are to do the same. And so are we. Not stressed out and pressure packed—but in peace.

So, let it sink in, these words are the apex and conclusion of the life of Jesus on earth. They are last for a reason. The final words and wishes of a father, on his death bed, weigh heavily on his sons and daughters. The "last will and testament" of an individual brings together everyone connected to him/her so a legal distribution of all possessions and property might occur. These words are Jesus' "last will and testament" for His followers. Of what importance have they been to you? Where in your list of daily priorities does God's will stand? One reason that the Great Commission is **great** because it is His **last** command!

The ONE accomplishment Jesus is looking for

Our second argument is this: during the last week of His life, the Passover Week, Jesus predicted woe on the scribes and Pharisees, upon Jerusalem, and upon the great temple there. He wept over Jerusalem after these predictions (Matthew 23:1-39.) He further predicted that the temple's destruction would be total as "there will not be left here one stone upon another that will not be thrown down" (Matt 24:2). This awful destruction was fulfilled in 70 AD.

Following these dire predictions, His disciples met with Him in a private session and asked Him: "Tell us when will these things be, and what will be the sign of your coming and of the end of the age?" (Matthew 24:3). In His lengthy answer, Jesus included these words,

> "And this gospel of the kingdom will be proclaimed throughout the whole world as a testimony to all nations, and then the end will come" (Matthew 24:14).

Jesus links the end of the age with the global proclamation of the gospel! He does **not** say that the end will come when Christians

(1) perfect their worship

(2) read through the Bible in a year

(3) become the most philanthropic power on earth

(4) learn to pray without ceasing

(5) overturn Roe v. Wade[44]

(6) join together in biblical unity[45]

(7) settle their theological disputes

(8) reach perfect holiness and stop falling into sin

(9) return to a family-based focus

(10) treat all of their opponents in perfect love

This list could go on. Everything on it, in my opinion, is good, and would bring a blessing if fulfilled. In fact, I have worked in some way towards every goal listed. However, **none of these are the turning point of future history.** Jesus returns and establishes His earthly kingdom when the gospel of the kingdom is universally proclaimed!

So, if that is the **one great goal** that Jesus is looking for, is it your first priority? Is sharing the soul-saving gospel in love your greatest goal on a daily basis? If it is, and if you follow His disciple making strategy, you will have plenty of opportunities

---

[44] The horrific US Supreme Court decision in 1973 which legalized abortion in the USA

[45] Note that the reason Jesus prays "that they all may be one" is "so that the world may believe" (John 17:21). There is a missional reason beyond the glorious, objective unity of the Church. Our unity may be seen, so it is not primarily a "spiritual or invisible" unity that Jesus is praying for. How can the world see that? It can't!

to do so. You can make disciples and appear at the judgment seat before Him with "fruit that remains." But it would appear to me that to let our lives get absorbed with other things or issues not relevant to the salvation of the lost, is a dangerous departure from that which concerns Christ most.

One thing that Causes Angels in Heaven to Rejoice

Thirdly, Jesus gave His disciples and us a glimpse into heaven that both surprises and baffles.

> "What man among you, having a hundred sheep, if he has lost one of them, does not leave the ninety-nine in the open country, and go after the one that is lost until he finds it? And when he has found it, he lays it on his shoulders, rejoicing. And when he comes home, he calls together his friends and his neighbors saying to them, 'Rejoice with me, for I have found my sheep that was lost.' **Just so, I tell you, there will be more joy in heaven over one sinner who repents than over ninety-nine righteous persons who need no repentance.** (Luke 15:3-7).

He then tells a similar story about a woman who loses a coin. His revelation about heaven is even more startling at the close of that parable. "Just so, I tell you, there is joy before the angels of God over one sinner who repents" (Luke 15:10).

Dear Christian reader, what makes you rejoice? I mean really **makes** you happy. Something that you cannot control yourself from delighting in? Your treasure found will **make** you break out with obvious joy! Whether it is a lost sheep, or coin, or car keys or credit card or…

But, what about a lost soul being found? When you hear of that or, better, experience it as a fruit of your prayer and work, do you get uncontrollably gleeful? For a long time? If not, I can offer a few responses:

-You may have forgotten the sweetness of your own salvation

-You may have grown skeptical over alleged conversions because you have seen so many of them fizzle out

-You may have misplaced your real treasure and substituted it with something worldly because "where your treasure is, there your heart will be also" (Matt 6:19)

-You were never really all that excited about your own salvation because you know that it really did not change your heart

Whatever the reason may be, dear friend, REPENT! You must know that if God's angels rejoice over one sinner being found, **something must be tragically wrong when your life and work do not focus on that one thing!**

Why do you look forward to "going to heaven" when you will die, if you are not rejoicing in heaven's delight here and now? It makes no sense. And might this not even reveal that you do not belong there? That you would be more at home among those whose lives are focused solely on their own miserable lives! If we choose to focus mainly on ourselves while we live on earth, will we really be "at home" in heaven when our lives will be absorbed in the adoration of God and love for all beings there?

Or are you banking on such a transformation at death that you will hardly be recognizable? That, dear friend, is a most risky assumption! The many words and warnings of God that I have brought forward to you in this little book are all designed to prepare you for life with God by joining with Him in your lives on earth!

If you are truly born again and have really received Him, it was "not of blood, nor of the will of the flesh, nor of the will of man—**but of God**" (John 1:13). What God gives birth to is godly or God-like! And there is nothing on earth more like

Jesus than seeking to save the lost. "For the Son of Man came to seek and to save the lost" (Luke 19:10). How can you be His follower and not follow in obeying His final command – Go and make disciples?

Declaring the gospel and making disciples was His final command. Its universal proclamation is the one thing that will trigger His return. And its fruit is the joy of heaven. When the Holy Spirit fills you, sharing your faith and making disciples will be your joy, too. Believe this, surrender daily to Christ, and be filled with the Spirit! And if you need me or our team to help you take sincere steps in becoming a disciple who makes disciples, do not hesitate to contact me.[46] Be fruitful not unfruitful because, as we have seen, it really matters!

Why it Really Matters
Questions for Reflection (R) and ACTION (A)

1. What do you now think is really revealed about the heart of any Christian who can ignore Christ's Final Command? (R)

2. Can you repeat the 3 final, strong arguments in favor of our premise – believers are born to reproduce?

3. Please make certain that if you did not read the Appendices while going through this book, that you read through them now. (R)

4. Write to me and tell me how this book has affected you (A)

---

[46] at ed.gross@comcast.net. You may also follow our ministry at www.disciplesgo.com and friending us on FaceBook at edwardngross.

Appendix 1

Jesus and every New Testament writer expected their readers to actively share their faith

Here is a list of some of Christ's disciples, who "got it." They were born to reproduce, so many of them *immediately* shared their new-found faith with others. The impact of doing this quickly is that disciples begin to bond with Jesus by faith. They learn that He really "is with them until the end of the age," as they are constantly "going" and "making disciples." To **NOT** go will mean that the disciple will not initially bond with Jesus, but likely, with someone else—a fellow Christian or their church. Just as in birth, a physical imprinting occurs through the quick bonding process of mother and offspring, so in spiritual re-birth, the disciple must bond with Jesus. Since He is not physically present, this cohesion occurs by an obedient faith. If Jesus says, "GO," the disciple must go. The only way to "follow" Jesus, who is always on the move advancing His Kingdom, is to get moving with Him. Paul knew this and, so, advised Philemon: **"I pray that you may be active in sharing your faith, so that you will have a full understanding of every good thing we have in Christ" (Philemon 6-NIV).**

-Andrew, immediately goes and tells Peter and brings him to Jesus (John 1:40-42)

-Philip finds Nathanael and invites him to "come and see" (John 1:43-50)

-Levi (Matthew) leaves his tax collecting, follows Jesus and immediately hosts a banquet at his home, inviting many others to come and meet Jesus (Mark 2:13-17; Luke 5:27-32)

-Jesus chooses 12 Apostles from His disciples, "so that they might be with him and he might send them out to preach (Mark 3:14)

-The Samaritan woman believes and immediately tells the whole town, who also believed (John 4:39-42)

-The man healed from "a legion" of demons wants to follow Jesus, but He, instead, immediately sends him to tell family and friends about God and His mercy (Mark 5:18-20)

-Jesus sends out His apostles two by two (Mark 6:7-13)

-Jesus sends out "72 others" (Luke 10:1-20)

-Zacchaeus believes and tells Jesus, leaders and other tax collectors, "Half of my goods I give to the poor" (Luke 19:1-10)

-One of the crucified criminals believes and warns the other criminal (Luke 23:39-43)

-11 disciples, some doubting, commanded to GO and make disciples! (Matt 28:16-20)

-The 120 are filled with the Spirit and begin to tell "the mighty works of God" in languages that they have never learned! (Acts 2:1-11)

-Peter immediately shares the gospel and 3000 are saved (Acts 2:14-40)

The healed lame man immediately joins Peter and John as he "praises God" (Acts 3:1-8)

-The 12 apostles are rescued from prison and told to immediately go to the temple and "speak all the words of this Life," which they do, though previously forbidden by the Sanhedrin to speak. (Acts 5:20-21)

-The Jerusalem Church (except the apostles) are scattered by persecution and they "went about preaching the word" (Acts 8:1-4)

-Saul converted on road to Damascus, filled with the Spirit, "immediately proclaimed Jesus in the synagogues" (Acts 9:1-20)

-Cornelius and others are converted and immediately filled with the Spirit and "extolling God" in unlearned languages (Acts 10:44-46)

-Barnabas and Saul, "sent out by the Holy Spirit... proclaimed the word of God" (Acts 13:1-5)

-12 Ephesians get saved and immediately begin "speaking in languages they had never learned and prophesying" (Acts 19:1-7)

-The whole church of Rome declared to be "filled with all knowledge and able to instruct one another" (Rom 15:14). They were all included in the manner that God normally saves the unconverted by the sobering logic of Paul, who wrote, "How will they call on him in whom they have not believed? And how are they to believe in him of whom they have never heard? And how are they to hear without someone preaching?" (Rom 10:14-15)

-The Corinthian believers are commanded, "Wake up from your drunken stupor, for some have no knowledge of God, I say this to your shame" (1 Cor 15:34)

-The Galatian church is criticized as those who are "so quickly deserting him who called you in the grace of Christ and are turning to a different gospel" (Gal 1:6)

-To the whole Ephesian church is committed "the work of ministry" and they were commanded to "speak the truth in love" (Eph. 4:12,15)

-The entire Philippian church is to keep bearing witness and "shine as light in the world, holding fast to the word of life" (Phil 2:15-16)

-The Colossian church (whom Paul had never met (2:1), is commanded "Let your speech always be gracious, seasoned with salt, so that you may know how to answer each person" (Col 4:5-6)

-The Thessalonians witness so powerfully that Paul commends them as his "model" church, "For not only has the word of the Lord sounded forth from you in Macedonia and Achaia, but your faith in God has gone for the everywhere, so that we need not say anything" (1 Thess 1:7-8)

-The letter to Hebrew believers chides them for being quieted by persecution because, instead, they all "ought to be teachers" (Hebrews 5:12)

-James, writing to the dispersed people of God, concludes his letter saying, "My brothers, if anyone among you wanders from the truth and someone brings him back, let him know that whoever brings back a sinner from his wandering will save his soul from death and will hide a cover a multitude of sins" (James 5:19-20)

-Peter writes to all the "elect exiles" that they should all be "prepared to make a defense to anyone who asks you for a reason for the hope that is in you; yet do it with gentleness and respect" (1 Peter 3:15)

-John writes to all believers, "Whoever confesses that Jesus is the son of God, God abides in him, and he in God" (1 John 4:15)

-Jude writes to all "called, beloved in God the Father and kept for Jesus Christ" (v. 1), that they should "have mercy on those who doubt; save others snatching them out of the fire" (v. 22-23)

-And in the final New Testament book, Jesus reveals and John writes about all those who will overcome the devil in these words, "And they have conquered him by the blood of the Lamb and by the word of their testimony, for they loved not their lives even unto death" (Rev. 12:11)

Appendix 2

Evangelism: then and now

Although this is not a how-to book on effective evangelism and discipleship, it would seem incomplete without saying something about them. Evangelicals have long evangelized. But, unfortunately, they have not often made disciples of those who responded to their gospel message. Instead, we have been taught to press them for a "decision." And that decision is best commenced through praying "the sinner's prayer." This would include some confession of sin, statement of faith in Christ and, then, asking Him "to come into one's heart." Sometimes this has led to a genuine follower of Jesus being made. But not often, because our invitation and procedure have little or nothing to do with making them a disciple or consecrated follower of Jesus. We have looked mainly for faith in words and have not called for faith in action, as Jesus and the first disciples did. As a result, many respond who have no intention of surrendering their lives and following Jesus.

Throughout the world, missionaries and leaders are forsaking this consumer-driven model of evangelism, aimed chiefly with helping others escape hell quickly and easily. I would really recommend your reading chapter 13 of Jerry Trousdale's book, Miraculous Movements: How Hundreds of Thousands of Muslims are Falling in Love with Jesus. The biblical and contemporary way of making disciples who make disciples is simply portrayed in that fascinating book. I would also recommend Jim Lilly's book, *Great Commission Disciple Making* as a very helpful step-by-step guide in how to evangelize and make disciples in one process.

My other recent books all deal with aspects of how to help Christians become disciples who make disciples. In fact, this is the main focus of our ministry globally. Churches are in great decline and do not know their way out.

My advice would be to **study Luke 10:1-12** and apply it as closely as possible to your life and context. This describes how Jesus sent 72 out in preparation. He showed them and trained them before He sent them out globally to make disciples. He taught and trained them in a very specific order how to effectively disciple others. This includes:

1. Prayer that leads to His guiding them "into the harvest"

2. "Go" totally trusting Him, staying focused on the call to connect with His prepared "person of peace.

3. Enter every situation with the prayer "peace be to this place." He promised that such a prayer in faith would link us with a readied, receptive "person of peace." Their lives are normally marked by receptivity, responsiveness and openness.

4. Start a Spirit-taught DBS (Discovery Bible Study) with the person of peace and anyone else he/she has invited "to discover God," too.

5. Grow the group through the witness of the people of peace who will share the story with others and will begin responding to God's conviction by doing "I Will Statements" weekly, flowing naturally from the DBS.

The organization with which I am connected, CityNet Ministries, as well as several others can provide training in how to facilitate a DBS group and how and when to multiply. One great personal resource is Fred Hall. Contact him at fredericklhall@hotmail.com

The main problem we are encountering in the USA is a reticence or reluctance of Christians to connect with strangers. In my opinion, this is a love problem. We will go, connect, listen well and have Holy Spirit guidance **only if we are filled with His love.**

Picture it like this: God is love (1 John 4:8). Jesus is God. Therefore, Jesus is love. If true discipleship is "following Jesus," then true discipleship is following love. Put another way—Jesus will lead you where only love can take you. We don't witness because we are not filled with the love of God.

We have helped train 1000's in the USA and globally in "how to make disciples who make disciples." BUT how many of those who have been trained are successfully making disciples? Only those who are filled with the Spirit and love of God on a daily basis! Only those who, see the multitudes today as Jesus did in His day— "When he saw the crowds he had compassion for them because they were harassed and helpless, like sheep without a shepherd" (Matt. 9:36). Love will lead us to help the hopelessly lost ones around us.

That is why this book is as much for those who understand New Testament discipleship as those who only understand traditional western evangelism. Nothing matters if you do not connect with people of peace! The Lord of the harvest will lead you "into the harvest." Christ will connect you to those whom He has made receptive. BUT you have to want to connect. You must stop staying and doing something in isolation. You have to move out. You have to "go" in love for anything to happen.

The life of the NT Church was a life on the move. Sometimes by design and sometimes by persecution. "Now those who were scattered (by persecution) went everywhere proclaiming the gospel" (Acts 8:4 – my translation). God uses conflicts. Sometimes we go by a strategic determination that it is the will of God to leave one place and go to another. "While they were worshiping the Lord and fasting, the Holy Spirit said, 'Set apart for me Barnabas and Saul for the work to which I have called them'" (Acts 13:2). The power of NT era evangelism was that disciples were available to be led out by the Spirit. And they obeyed!

When you go and share the gospel, make sure that it is always connected with a proper call to response. "Repent and believe the gospel" is the most often form in the mouths of Jesus and His disciples. Repentance always signifies both confession (a sound) and discipleship (a look). It sounds like, "Forgive me! I am sorry for my sin!" It looks like following Jesus. Jesus will lead you away from a life of sin.

When He called the lost, Jesus repeatedly said, "If anyone would come after me, let him deny himself and take up his cross daily and follow me. For whoever would save his life will lose it, but whoever would save his life fort my sake will save it. For what does it profit a man if he gains the whole world and loses or forfeits himself? (Luke 9:23-25, etc).

Jesus' invitation demanded a true cost calculation by the responder. Self-denial, cross carrying, forfeiture of one's dreams and will were the doors through which the repentant sinner goes to find life in Christ. It is the same today! Do not make it easy on them. You cannot chase away one whom the Spirit of God is drawing to faith! That is a major difference between evangelism then and evangelism now.

The call to salvation includes the call to discipleship. So, out of necessity, we must be ready to connect the new believer with a discipler. Otherwise we are calling merely for a decision which might end up either in it lasting or failing.

Please understand that we are not serving anyone well by merely calling for a "profession of faith." The Great Commission is – Go and make disciples![47]

---

[47] See Appendix Two in my "Are You a Christian or a Disciple?' for a report on the very important 1999 International Consultation on Discipleship – which tried to address the problem of Evangelicalism's producing 1000's of converts but very few disciples.

Appendix 3

No GOING without being SENT - *PEACEFULLY*

One of the problems of much of today's Christian "witnessing" is that it is coerced from guilt and not motivated by the love of God. We often witness because we are shamed into it. Others are going to hell, so we MUST tell them of Christ, whether they want to listen or not! We are pressured and we pressure them. And, so usually we do a poor job as we try to pressure others to believe. Doesn't this feel wrong to you?

It is. You see, Jesus is the Prince of Peace. And He said, "Peace be with you. As the Father has sent me, even so I am sending you" (John 20:21). The God who is in control, wants us to so trust Him that we never lose our peace! Even when He sends us out "as lambs in the midst of wolves" (Luke 10:3). He is the One who said, "All authority in heaven and on earth has been given to me. Go therefore and make disciples…And behold, I am with you to the end of the age" (Matthew 28:18-20). His Presence is the KEY. He is the One in control! He is "the Lord of the harvest" to whom we pray before we go (Luke 10:2).

Many disciples whom we have trained forget this crucial point—and fail as a result. They "master" the material, the form of leading a Discovery Bible Studies (DBS)—and wrongly think that they are thereby ready. Nothing makes us ready to face the world, the flesh and the devil except utter and complete trust in the presence of Jesus!

Why doesn't Satan destroy us on this mission? We are opposing him and his kingdom, taking from him those who have served him. Listen carefully:

> "Little children, you are from God and have overcome them, for he who is in you is greater than he who is in the world…. We know that everyone who is born of God does not keep on sinning, but he who was born of God

(Jesus) protects him, and the evil one does not touch him. We know that we are from God, and the whole world lies in the power of the evil one." (1 John 4:4, 18-19).

We are not destroyed because God is with us. We no longer live under the power of sin because the Spirit of God has freed us from it. Satan cannot even "touch" us when we walk with Jesus by a true, living faith. When we are "going" through the day with Him. As Brother Lawrence says, when we are "practicing the presence of God."

BUT, having said all that—here is my main point: people stop going when they lose the conscious belief that Jesus is personally with them as the Sender! Every day we must view Him as sending us and going with us. Otherwise, we will be swamped by the realities of the physical world and its Christ-opposing philosophies and cultures.

Listen to Paul's inspired logic and think of a chain. He starts with the outcome: "everyone who calls on the name of the Lord will be saved" (Romans 10:13). Then he works backwards, going link-by-link over the chain that has led them to Christ. "How then will they call on him in whom they have not believed? (they won't). And how are they to believe in him of whom they have never heard? (they won't). And how are they to hear without someone preaching? (they won't). And how are they to preach unless they are sent? (they won't)." (Romans 10:14-15). I have added the "they won'ts" because that is the unstated but understood meaning of each rhetorical question, or link in the chain.

So, if the chain has one link broken, the chain is broken and the end will not likely happen. I am seeing that, even after training others all about New Testament discipleship one-on-one or through a group RBD (Renewal of Biblical Discipleship). Even after giving them the tools of how to start a DMM (Disciple Making Movement) prayer time, connect with a "person of peace," facilitate a DBS (Discovery Bible

Study), and even understand healing prayer—many are not effectively making disciples!!! Why? Why do they stop after starting? Why do they grow discouraged along the way and give up?

Theologically they know they need the daily empowering of the Spirit and are seeking it. BUT here is the missing link— they do NOT see themselves as being SENT daily by Jesus into the harvest! How can they effectively preach (share) the gospel unless they are sent? They can't!! Every day is unique and so special. You are the sower and, in season, reaper—by His helping grace and Spirit.

That is the reason this appendix is so vital. To urge you to connect your "going" with your being "sent." You see, Jesus is with you. That is why Satan and all his wolves cannot touch you and deter you. Sure, Jesus will definitely allow you to sometimes experience suffering BUT only as a door that opens to further effective witness. Our crosses that we bear will all advance the kingdom if we bear them "in Christ" and not apart from Him.[48]

You will stick with the narrow path of discipling others only if you are inextricably united with Jesus. You must not let anyone or anything come between you and Him. Daily and moment-by-moment. He is sending you every day and throughout the day. So, be in that mindset as you go your way. Take Him with you, so to speak. And His peace will reign over you and flow through you to the people of peace He has prepared for you to disciple along the way.

I hope it is now obvious to you what I mean by the title: No GOING without being SENT – *Peacefully.*

---

[48] See my *"The Amazing Love of Paul's Model Church* chapter 3 entitled, "Paul, why were you beaten in Philippi?"

Appendix 4

Faith without <u>WHICH</u> works is dead?

The title of this book is "Fruitful or Unfruitful: Why it Really Matters." I have spent a good deal of time addressing what the Scriptures and Jesus often mean by "fruitful. " The main point of fruitfulness is reproduction. Many Christians, sadly, do not reproduce. But, all true disciples reproduce. Because that was one of the defining marks of a disciple—they duplicated![49]

James faced head-on the issue of Christians saying that they believed BUT did not possess the normal outcomes of true faith. Some were saying that all they wanted was to be accepted by God (justified), so they did not care how others viewed them. James insisted, by the Spirit, that true, justifying faith will NEVER stand alone in one's life. True faith is a living and productive thing. True faith WORKS, that is—it bears fruit. This is how he said it:

> "What good is it, my brothers, if someone says he has faith but does not have works? Can that faith save him? If a brother or sister is poorly clothed and lacking in daily food, and one of you says to them, 'Go in peace, be warmed and filled, 'without giving them the things needed for the body, what good is that? So also, faith by itself, if it does not have works, is dead. But someone will say, 'You have faith and I have works.' Show me your faith apart from your works and I will show you my faith by my works.' You believe that God is one; you do well. Even the demons believe – and shudder! ...For as the body apart from the spirit is dead, so faith apart from works is dead." (James 3:14-19,26)

---

[49] This is a major theme in my *Are You a Christian or a Disciple? Rediscovering and Renewing New Testament Discipleship*

Relevant to our focus would be this question—Did James believe that sharing the gospel and discipling or helping to save others—was one of the works or evidences of true faith? Or, could someone be a silent, solitary believer?

It is obvious, from the context itself, that James advances physically assisting a needy fellow believer as one of the fruits of faith. He also advances the obedience of Abraham when he "offered up Isaac on the altar" as another proof of what saving faith looks like (v. 21). And James also illustrated his point that true faith produces action by the dangerous and selfless act of Rahab "when she received the messengers and sent them out by another way" (v. 25).

Glancing through his letter, I see the following evidences that James expected all of his readers to be active in sharing their faith and reproducing spiritually:

> "Of his own will he brought us forth by the word of truth, that we should be a kind of firstfruits of his creatures. (1:18)

God has "birthed" us through the ministry of the word for the purpose that we should be in His creation what "firstfruits" were to a harvest. These reproductive and harvest expressions seem to imply that God had a goal of fruitfulness in mind when He saved us. The firstfruits were mature and reproducible. Ripe and ready to be used, eaten, planted. Are you ripe? Ready to reproduce?

> "But be doers of the word and not hearers only, deceiving yourselves" (1:22)

A doer is a producer. One who hears and obeys. We have to look no further than the Great Commission of our Lord to know that He has given us all this word: "Make disciples!" Are you a doer of this word or only a hearer? How many disciples have you made?

"If you really fulfill the royal law according to the Scripture, 'You shall love your neighbor as yourself,' you are doing well. But if you show partiality and you are committing sin and are convicted by the law as transgressors.... So speak and so act as those who are to be judged under the law of liberty. For judgment is without mercy to one who has shown no mercy. Mercy triumphs over judgment" (2:8,9,12,13).

Our actions and speech are to selflessly serve our neighbor's true need. And, according to the context, there is no greater need than to be merciful. Mercy is a special kind of love. It is love for those who are in a pitiful state. Are you moving towards your needy neighbors in both deeds and words of love? Do you show and share the gospel of God's precious saving love?

The greatest sin of omission

"So whoever knows the right thing to do and fails to do it, for him it is sin" (4:18)

Is it right to keep the gospel and its eternal benefits to ourselves and allow our neighbors to perish? Is it right to leave the Great Commission unfulfilled in our lives? Is it right to bury the knowledge and blessings that we have and not put them to work in the harvest for the Master? Is it right to say that we believe Jesus could come TODAY but not be working: sowing and reaping TODAY as if we believed He might come today? These questions elicit from us all the same answers. Let us repent and not live in such sins of omission.

Why did the prophets suffer?

"Be patient, therefore, brothers until the coming of the Lord. See how the farmer waits for the precious fruit of the earth, being patient about it, until it receives the early and late rains. You also be patient. Establish your hearts, for the coming of the Lord is at hand.... As an example of suffering and patience, brothers, take the prophets who spoke in the name of the Lord. Behold, we consider those blessed who remained steadfast. (5:7-11)

Here is another illustration from farming. The farmer must be patient. Without patience there is no fruit. No harvest. And to what is James referring? To the believers patient, prophet-like sufferings! The prophets suffered because they spoke up. They shared an unpopular message. WHY? Because God had sent them to speak what the people needed to hear. Even if they did not want to hear it. The Early Church suffered because it spoke. It spoke because it was filled with the Spirit of God which gave them great love and boldness. Are you patiently speaking? Even when it causes suffering? Or do you refrain from speaking because it will bring suffering?

The last, great words of James

Please consider how James closes his letter. If one of his aims was to describe what true, saving faith looks like—read carefully his last words:

> "My brothers, if anyone among you wanders from the truth and someone brings him back, let him know that whoever brings back a sinner from his wandering will save his soul from death and will cover a multitude of sins" (5:19-20)

James is led by the Spirit to demand a faith that works. Paul wrote "For in Christ Jesus...the only thing that counts is faith expressing itself through love" (Gal 5:6). James leaves us with a picture of rescuing others from their sins. From death.

The brilliant Christian apologist, Ravi Zacharias, wrote, "Nobody is born a Christian. All Christians are such by virtue of conversion. To ask the Christian not to reach out to anyone else who is from another faith is to ask that Christian to deny his own faith."[50]

Yes! We deny the essence of our own powerfully converting faith when we do not seek the powerful conversion of others. We merely expect God to use us in others as He used someone else to lead us into life. So, we would conclude, that a reproductive or duplicating faith IS one of those fruits which James would consider as proving the possession of true faith. It is not the ONLY mark of a saved person; but, it is an important product of true faith. This is one reason why it really matters that you share the gospel and make disciples of the Lord.

---

[50] Ravi Zacharias in *Jesus Among Other Gods*, 158.

Appendix 5

Christians should FEAR standing before God unfruitfully

Many today want nothing to do with "the fear of the Lord." They quote 1 John 4:18, "There is no fear in love, but perfect love casts out fear." They should finish quoting that verse which continues "For fear has to do with punishment, and whoever fears has not been perfected in love." That is the whole verse. Notice that John is referring to a very specific fear, the fear of judgment. A loving walk with Jesus drives out the fear of condemnation.

But does it eliminate all fear? Of course not! Fear is a natural emotion. Part of our created nature. Fear may be a very good thing. Fear keeps us from crossing the road without looking. Fear leads many to evacuate their beloved homes and priceless property when a Category 4 hurricane is heading their way. Fear keeps a husband from adultery, knowing what could happen to his marriage if he is found out. Fear keeps a child from letting go of his mother's hand.

Solomon wisely said, "The fear of the Lord is the beginning of knowledge; fools despise wisdom and instruction" (Proverbs 1:7). There is a reason why that proverb was chosen to be the first proverb in the Book of Proverbs! When Paul was listing the sins which capture the hearts of humans and constitute their cultures, he made their ultimate sin, this awful characteristic: "There is no fear of God before their eyes" (Romans 3:9-18).

In his masterpiece, John Calvin concludes his first chapter addressing the natural fear of God that humans experience whenever they are brought into the pure presence of their infinite, eternal and almighty God.

"Hence that dread and amazement with which, as Scripture uniformly relates, holy men were struck and overwhelmed whenever they beheld the presence of God. When we see those who previously stood firm and secure, so quaking with terror, that the fear of death takes hold of them... the inference is to be drawn is, that men are never duly touched and impressed with a conviction of their insignificance, until they have contrasted themselves with the majesty of God."[51]

The same apostle who wrote 1 John 4:18 also recorded,

"Then I turned to see the voice that was speaking to me...one like a son of man, clothed with a long robe and with a golden sash around his chest. The hairs of his head were white, like white wool, like snow. His eyes were like a flame of fire, his feet were like burnished bronze, refined in a furnace, and his voice was like the roar of many waters. and his face was like the sun shining in full strength. **When I saw him, I fell at his feet as though dead.** But he laid his right hand on me, saying, 'Fear not, I am the first and the last....'" (Revelation 1:12-17)

When humans behold the glory of God, they are often portrayed as falling down, covering their eyes, their heads, in fear. It was only when Jesus touched John and told him not to fear, that he could continue. Whenever we, the creatures, meet our glorious Creator, there is an immediate "attitude adjustment." We are humbled before Him. And everything takes a different perspective. There is a reason why every knee will bow and every tongue will confess that Jesus Christ is Lord to the glory of God the Father (Phil 2: 10-11). That is simply stating that the day is coming when the truth of who Jesus is will be universally known!

Until that day, it is good to "walk humbly with your God" (Micah 6:8). And part of that humility is understanding a bit of

---

[51] John Calvin, *The Institutes of the Christian Religion*, *chap 1, par 3, page 39.*

the glory and power of our Triune God. So, one Bible writer, when discussing the coming judgment, reminded us, "It is a fearful thing to fall into the hands of the living God" (Hebrews 10:31).

Unfortunately, today, there seems to be little fear of God among Christians. This might also be a reason why so few bear a bold and fruitful witness of Christ. Paul linked the fear of the Lord with being an effective Christian witness when he wrote, "Therefore, knowing the fear of the Lord, we persuade others" (2 Corinthians 5:11).

Please note the warning to those who know God's saving truth and do not share it:

> "If you falter in times of trouble, how small is your strength! Rescue those being led away to death; hold back those staggering towards slaughter. If you say, 'But we knew nothing about this,' does not he who weighs the heart perceive it? Does not he who guards your life know it? Will he not repay each person according to what he has done?" (Proverbs 24:10-12 – NIV)

> "Son of man, I have made you a watchman for the house of Israel. Whenever you hear a word from my mouth, you shall give them warning from me. If I say to the wicked, 'You shall surely die,' and you give him no warning…in order to save his life, that wicked person shall die for his iniquity, but his blood I will require at your hand. But if you warn the wicked and he does not turn from his wickedness…he shall die for his iniquity, but you will have delivered your soul." (Ezekiel 3:16-19)

> "Son of man, speak to your people and say to them, If I bring the sword upon a land, and the people of the land take a man from among them and make him their watchman, and if he sees the sword coming upon the land and blows the trumpet and warns the people, then if anyone who hears the sound of the trumpet does not take

warning, and the sword comes and takes him away, his blood shall be upon his own head. He heard the sound of the trumpet, and did not take warning; his blood shall be upon himself. But if he had taken warning, he would have saved his life. But if the watchman sees the sword coming and does not blow the trumpet, so that the people are not warned, and the sword comes and takes any one of them, that person is taken away in his iniquity, but his blood will I require at watchman's hand. So you, son of man, I have made a watchman.... If you warn the wicked to turn from his way, and he does not turn...that person shall die in his iniquity, but you will have delivered your soul'" (Ezekiel 33:2-9).

Please do not quickly say— "But he is a prophet. Or, that is Old Testament, Old Covenant terms. I am under the New Covenant." It is not quite that easy to exonerate yourself. When he was speaking to the Ephesian elders for the last time, Paul reminded them,

> "And now, behold I know that none of you among whom I have gone about proclaiming the kingdom will see my face again. Therefore, I testify to you this day that I am innocent of the blood of all, for I did not shrink from declaring to you the whole counsel of God. (Acts 20:25-27) And when he spoke to the resistant Jews in Corinth, he declared, "Your blood be on your own heads! I am innocent. From now on I will go to the Gentiles." (Acts 18:6).

Paul spoke of blood on his hands. Though not often used today, we know what that means. It means to be responsible or culpable for the injury or death of another. Paul, the great advocate of the New Covenant, states that his ministry would demand the strictest account before God. He saw his call as having "life and death" consequences. Not only to his hearers. But, also to himself. From where did Paul take his terminology? No doubt from the Old Testament prophets.

When we know disaster is coming and do not "blow the trumpet" in warning to others, will we be held responsible? This whole book cries out, "YES!" Of course, it is not my place to say what the nature of those consequences will be. But, Scripture clearly portrays that they will be serious! James warned, "So whoever knows the right thing to do and fails to do it, for him it is sin" (James 4:17)

If you were the Father and you had sent your blessed Son to die for the sins of humankind. What would you think if those your Son died to save refused to share that Good News with other dying sinners? What would you do to them?

The Lord warned quite explicitly, "For whoever is ashamed of me and my words, of him will the Son of Man be ashamed when he comes in his glory and the glory of his Father and of the holy angels." (Luke 9:26).

Note the bold witness of the many believers in the Book of the Revelation, a book concerning what was past, present and future—with relevance to all:

> "When he opened the fifth seal, I saw under the altar the souls of those who had been slain for the word of God and for the witness they had borne" (Rev. 6:9)

> "And they conquered him (Satan) by the blood of the Lamb and by the word of their testimony, for they loved not their lives even unto death" (Rev. 12:11)

> "And I saw the woman, drunk with the blood of the saints, the blood of those who bore testimony to Jesus" (Rev. 17:6)

Do you really think it is safe to have a way of life that simply does not fit the one depicting the victorious believers in the Book of the Revelation?

www.ingramcontent.com/pod-product-compliance
Lightning Source LLC
Chambersburg PA
CBHW052149110526
44591CB00012B/1914